SPECIAL PLACES

Washington State's Top 40 Independent Places to Stay
for

Romance, Adventure
and
Gourmet Cuisine

By Mardi and Fred Nystrom

Sun Mountain Lodge

Acknowledgements

Special recognition should go to Mae West who summed up our approach to life in her famous quote

"Too much of a good thing can be wonderful."

To our daughter Makenna who has endured numerous trips with us over the years, as she readies herself (and us) for her solo trip off to WSU where she will turn out for the rowing team.

Special Credits
Design and Layout—Amanda Predmore, Keli Fujioka, Elements of Design
Editorial Development—Nancy Atkins and Kate Kirby
Proofing—Makenna Nystrom and Alex Jones
Printing—Printing Control Graphics

Photographic Contributions
Brad Schmidt Photography—P6
Michael Jensen—P12-13
David Conklin—P22-23
Stewart Hopkins—P24
Pam Merrill—P26
Stadler Studio—P42-43, 94
Gary Kleysteuber—P46
Tori Lenze—P47
Danny Wayne Lauve, TLD Pro Imagery—P48-49
Alicia Carlson—P53
Danny Wayne Lauve-TLD Pro Imagery—P64-65
Ben Benschneider—P70, 94
Don Portman—P74
Tom Burt—P75
Brian Gaines Photography—P80-81
Robb Drake, Plateau Portraits—back cover

ISBN 0-936777-05-2
Printed in Washington, USA

Rates shown in this edition are correct at the time of printing. Please note that all rates are subject to change without prior notice. For the most up-to-date information, please go to www.SpecialPlaces.com.

Mardi and I started our quest to discover the very best independent small hotels, B&Bs, restaurants and recreation providers way back in the early 1980's. We started to travel extensively together, applying her restaurant experience with my background at Sunset magazine. We quickly learned that truly high-quality places were few and far between. So, for the next 20-years our research for Special Places publications took us around all the Western States and the entire Eastern seaboard. Today, we are able to stay close to home and have found a number of exceptional places to stay right here in Washington.

During the past few years the leisure travel market has radically changed. With gas prices soaring and air travel a painful experience; people are now taking shorter, more frequent vacations closer to home. To help you find the hidden jewels right here in Washington, Mardi and I have researched and selected the "Top 40" places in the state to be in this book. We know they are the best since we have visited hundreds of places to select these 40.

Why Buy a Book When the Internet is Free?
The Internet is like a giant library, but most travel sites can't afford to visit even a fraction of the places they feature so they rely on "consumer generated copy, " encouraging any and every one to comment on their experiences. This results in a hodge-podge review process and the reader can never know if the commentator is employed by the property or has even been there. That is a dicey way to gather reliable information for your trips.

This *Special Places* book is a search engine in print. We have spent the time and effort to visit each place and what we have to say is accurate, realistic and viewed through the eye of a travel professional. If you want to experience the best lodging, dining and recreational opportunities in Washington, then this should be your guide.

What makes a place "Special"?
It is all about the hosting. AAA and Mobil rate the quality of the building(s), but we feel strongly that this is not the whole story. While we inspect the facilities, we pay a lot more attention to the owner and the staff and how they interact with their guests. A wonderful host can deliver world class hospitality in a relatively undistinguished physical space, while a person lacking in hospitality will bungle the experience even in a perfectly-designed facility. This personal approach to hospitality is the hallmark of all the places in this book. No amount of money invested in a property can ever take the place of inspired, from-the-heart hosting

How Do You Find These Special Places?
We find these places the old-fashioned way, by getting in the car and driving around to personally inspect the physical merits of each prospective place and to interact with the hosts. We travel incognito and pay for all services received.

Keep Informed
Please visit our web site at www.SpecialPlaces.com to find our all-time favorites and our latest selections, to purchase the newest books and get the inside information and value. Be certain to see the information on page 90 about the Association of Special Travelers program.

TABLE OF CONTENTS

BY MAP ICON & PAGE NUMBER

By Alphabetical Listing of Properties

MOUNTAIN HOME LC

Pet Friendly:
The property accepts pets under certain conditions and limitations. These conditions vary widely, so always verify with the property before your arrival.

Suitable for Children:
In general the more romantic and couples orientated the place, the less likely they want any children romping through the public rooms. Some properties accept children in the same room up to a certain age, while others only accept children over a certain age, so it is always good to check when making your reservation.

Meeting Facilities:
The property has the space and the amenities to provide for meetings. Amenities usually include tables, chairs and a quiet area. Larger facilities have more expansive meeting areas and services.

Fireplaces:
Fireplaces are available in at least some of the lodging rooms.

Handicapped Accessible:
Modifications have been made to allow safe access to common areas to at least one lodging room. Some of the older structures are ADA exempt and can not safely be remodeled to facilitate full handicapped access. If the icon is not shown, please check with the host to see if your specific requirements might still be safely met.

Internet Connections:
Connectivity will vary widely from a dial up to broadband and from a computer to wireless, so check based on your specific requirements.

Pool: A swimming pool open to the guests of the facility, this may also include a hot tub in addition to the pool.

Restaurant Open to the Public: While all palaces provide some level of food service to guests, certain places also accommodate non-guests for meals. These are generally country inns and larger more full-service hotels.

Spa Services:
This can range from a masseuse to a full-service spa facility.

Totally non-smoking Indoors: While this is becoming the standard, some of the larger facilities may still have a few smoking rooms, or in the case of a casino, a part of the casino may allow smoking.

Wedding Facilities:
They have both the facilities and the interest in hosting a wedding. Some places require the entire facility to be rented.

Workout Facilities:
The property has facilities on site for exercise or they have a special relationship with a full-service nearby gym for guests to use.

Washington State

Property names can be found on page 5 (Table of Contents)

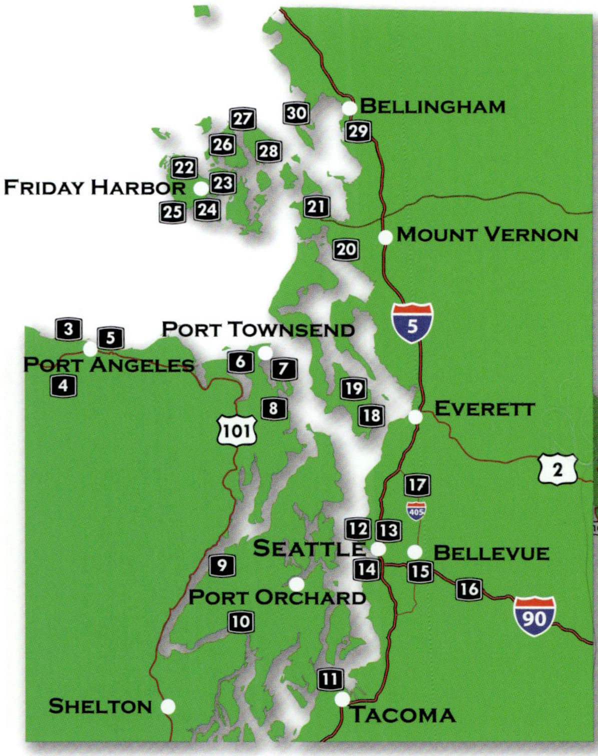

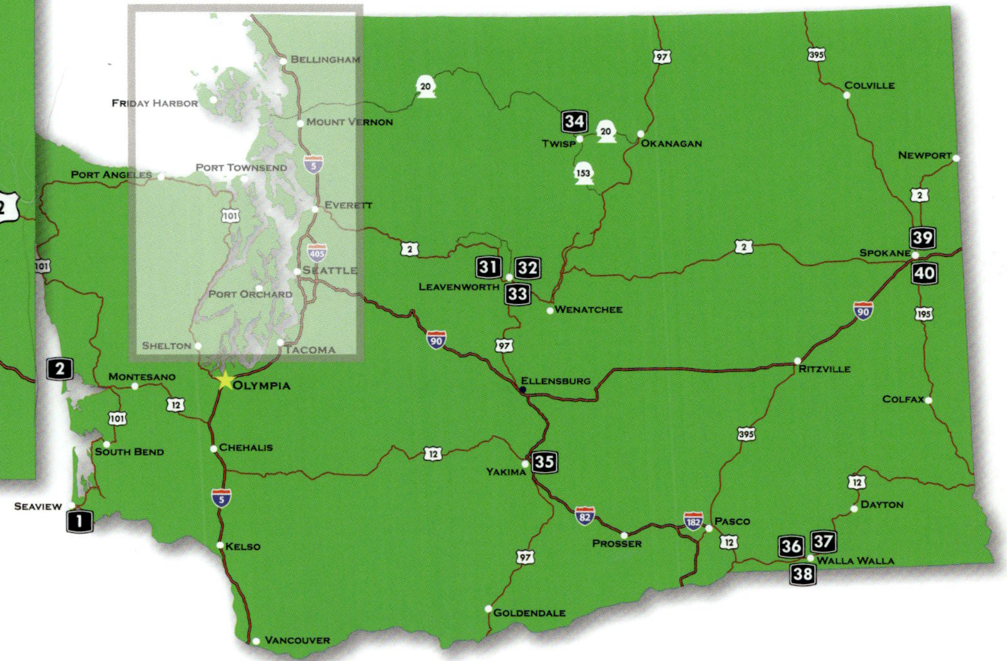

LOCATION: SEAVIEW 98644
ADDRESS: 4415 PACIFIC WAY SEAVIEW
HOSTS: DAVID CAMPICHE & LAURIE ANDERSON
PHONE: 360.642.2442
TOLL FREE: 800.466.1896
EMAIL: FRONTDESK@THESHELBURNEINN.COM
WEB SITE: WWW.THESHELBURNEINN.COM
ROOMS: 15
RATES: $135–$195
REMARKS: "IF YOU WANT TO SEE REAL PROFESSIONALS IN THE ART OF HOSTING AND LOOKING AFTER THEIR GUESTS, ALL YOU HAVE TO DO IS WATCH DAVID AND LAURIE DURING THE BREAKFAST HOURS. THEIR GENUINE CARING IS THE HALLMARK OF THEIR 30-YEARS OF RUNNING THE SHELBURNE."

If your romantic getaway includes walks on the beach, waves breaki over jetties and a lighthouse to add drama to your pictures, you'l find the Shelburne Inn to be the ultimate coastal experience.

Located on the gateway to the Lo Beach Peninsula in Seaview (just three blocks from the sand dunes the Shelburne Inn is the oldest continuously operating hotel in Washington. Established in 1896 (with additions made in 1911, 1983 and 1986), it is listed on the National Register of Historic Plac

Innkeepers and hosts David Campiche and Laurie Anderson have owned the inn since 1977.

The pair fell in love with the old building and have retained its historical charm while updating it and adding excellent food to the mix. With 30 years in the hospitality field, they are professional innkeepers who delight their guests with an attentive level of service while never intruding on their privacy.

If you're looking for something even more secluded, try their sister property China Beach Retreat. A Craftsman cottage nestled in a small cove at the mouth of the Columbia River in Ilwaco, it offers tideland views and puts you up close to the shorebirds navigating the tide flats. The Lewis and Clark expedition actually walked through the land on which China Beach now sits.

A Relaxing Retreat

The Shelburne Inn houses 15 guest rooms furnished with Victorian and Edwardian antiques. All have private bath and most offer a private deck. There are another two guest rooms and a suite at China Beach, plus the Audubon Cottage, (opened in late 2006) that offers an upstairs bedroom, 42" flat screen TV, two-person hydrotherapy tub plus an exterior deck downstairs with two-person soaking tub.

With freshly baked cookies upon your arrival, fresh flowers in the room, coffee and tea service all day, plus a computer for guests' use, you will feel pampered at every turn.

Award Winning Food and Drink

The innkeepers' award-winning breakfast is a command performance of traditional Pacific Northwest offerings (salmon, berries, wild mushrooms and edible greens) influenced with Scandinavian and Asian tastes. In particular, I especially enjoy David's omelets and Mardi looks forward to starting her day with Laurie's sourdough pancakes.

The nationally-acclaimed Shoalwater Restaurant onsite features gourmet dinners of fresh, locally harvested foods. Their wine cellar offers over 400 wines and has received many awards, including the Wine Spectator Award of Excellence.

For lighter fare, the more casual Heron & beaver Pub is a "mini-Cheers" offering over 40 beers/ciders plus over 20 wines by the glass. The Art Nouveau stained glass enclosing the restaurant and pub areas casts a beautiful light in the room, creating the perfect ambiance. Accessible from the pub is a deck overlooking the beautiful Victorian gardens of the Shelburne. A favorite spot of Mardi's, it's where we usually enjoy our dinner under one of the festive umbrellas

Before leaving the inn, we make it a ritual to visit the gift shop. In addition to being innkeepers, David is a potter and Laurie is a weaver and their selection of cookbooks, imported baskets, jewelry, antiques, textiles, small carvings and pottery (thrown by David himself) is an adventure all its own.

LOCATION: OCEAN SHORES 98569
—ON WASHINGTON COAST
ADDRESS: 78 STATE ROUTE (SR) 115
HOST: BOB SOUTHALL—GENERAL MANAGER
PHONE: 360.289.9466
TOLL FREE: 888.481.2214
EMAIL: INFO@QUINAULTBEACHRESORT.COM
WEB SITE: WWW.QUINAULTBEACHRESORT.COM
ROOMS: 159
RATES: $99.95–$179.95
REMARKS: " FINALLY WASHINGTON HAS AN OCEAN-FRONT RESORT TO MATCH THE BEAUTY AND SPLENDOR OF THIS MAJESTIC COASTLINE."

Abounding with shore birds, eagles and other wildlife, the Quinault Beach Resort and Casino is located on 250 acres of nature preserve overlooking the Pacific Ocean. It's also a fun and exciting place for a weekend that provides a balance of Las Vegas games with nature, a day spa and Native American culture.

Opened in 2000, the resort and casino are owned and operated by the Quinault Indian Nation, whic has lived in the area for 4,000 years. The resort is decorated in warm colors and casual style of a Northwest lodge architecture. Among its décor highlights are excellent examples of North Coast Indian artwork and artifacts.

Views of the Rolling Tide

The resort's 159 deluxe view rooms and suites all feel large and welcoming thanks to their 10-foot ceilings and friendly gas fireplaces with sitting areas. The French balconies overlook the ocean or a calming fountain. The king and queen pillow-topped mattresses offer a restful night's sleep. Among the various larger rooms are studio suites, with beautiful views of the wetlands and ocean beyond them, which may be enjoyed from the in-room whirlpool tubs.

The resort's most special feature may be either the 10,000 square foot casino... or the easy access to a sandy beach... or maybe it's the fact that the both are so accessible to each other, so you don't have to choose between them. The Las Vegas-style casino has keno, plus table games such as blackjack, craps, roulette and poker. The casino's claim to fame is that it has the only ocean-view Texas Hold 'Em poker room in Washington.

The resort offers a big indoor pool and exercise room, as well as a full-service day spa with treatments such as hot stone massage and mud facials. Adults and kids will also find fun outdoors on the easily accessible beach. Kite-flying and beachcombing are among the favorite activities, as is hiking in the Quinault Rain Forest and Olympic National Park. Also popular are deep-sea fishing, horseback riding and golfing, which are all nearby.

An Array of Dining Choices

Four restaurants provide delicious breakfasts, lunches and dinners. The flagship is Emily's Restaurant, which has been honored as the best fine dining restaurant in Grays Harbor County. Named after a tribal elder, Emily's serves fresh Northwest foods, with a focus on seafood. Naturally, the wild Northwest salmon is a house specialty, though the steaks are juicy from the grill. As for dessert, Mardi is a big fan of wild berries in puff pastry and fresh whipped cream. The elegant dining room is surrounded by hand-painted murals and delivers sweeping golden views of the ocean at sunset. Other food possibilities in the resort include sushi at Wasabi's Sushi Bar, light meals—and live entertainment—at the Ocean Lounge, and casual snacks and sandwiches at the Sidewalk Bistro.

The most remarkable part of a weekend at the Quinault Beach Resort and Casino is its ability to suit just about any mood, from relaxed to active, indoors to out. You don't have to choose ahead of time what you want to do for the weekend. And not having to decide may be the most relaxing possibility of all.

LOCATION: PORT ANGELES 98362 —ON NORTHERN OLYMPIC PENINSULA
ADDRESS: 339 FINN HALL ROAD
HOSTS: LYNDA & PETER CLARK
PHONE: 360.457.9197
TOLL FREE: 877.457.9777
EMAIL: COLETTES@COLETTES.COM
WEB SITE: WWW.COLETTES.COM
ROOMS: 5 GUESTROOMS AND SUITES
RATES: $175–$375
REMARKS: "THE VIEWS NORTH INTO BRITISH COLUMBIA ARE STUNNING."

Perched on a high bank overlooki the Strait of Juan de Fuca, Colett is a ten-acre estate nestled betwe the majestic Olympic Mountains and the Strait of Juan de Fuca. Every guest suite offers a sweepi panoramic ocean view of British Columbia, the San Juan Islands and Mount Baker. The magnifice oceanfront setting combined wit luxurious accommodations mak this secluded hideaway an ultima romantic retreat.

THE CASUAL ELEGANCE OF THE NORTHWEST

Hosts Lynda and Peter Clark have been entertaining guests in the Pacific Northwest for over 15 years. Their enthusiasm for the Northwest is complimented by the contemporary design of the inn and accented by Colette's collection of exceptional artwork by Pacific Northwest artists.

Built in 2000, this inn features a handsome great room and dining area illuminated by a 40-foot wall of windows with stunning views of the Strait of Juan de Fuca and the San Juan Islands. The handcrafted stone fireplace offers wonderful warmth and romantic firelight by day or night.

Mardi's and my favorite spot is on the main patio. It is a ritual of ours to relax there after a day of sightseeing at Hurricane Ridge (in nearby Olympic National Park). Feeling the glow of the outdoor fireplace as you watch the lights of Victoria, British Columbia sparkle across the water is a simple but romantic moment you'll remember forever.

Colette's Outdoor Sanctuary

The inn is a recent addition to the property, which, for over 55 years, has matured into lush gardens among the ancient cedar tree forests. With thousands of multi-colored vibrant flowering plants, and indigenous species paired with the exotic, this is simply a gardener's paradise. While we both enjoy gardening, we know these gardens are truly a labor of love on a very grand scale.

All the Elements: Fire, Water and Privacy

The suites are as wonderful as the gardens. All offer luxurious king beds, fireplaces, and Jacuzzi spas for two (situated to take in the ocean view). I especially appreciate the private patio which lets us go outside in the morning in our bathrobes to read the newspaper or sip a cup of coffee as we plan our day.

Colette's most private rooms are the Spruce Suite and Cedar Suite. Located right on the edge of an evergreen forest, you arrive there by following the meandering flagstone pathway through the fragrant fountain courtyard.

Breakfast and Beyond

Breakfast is a multi-course gourmet affair that combines regional flavors with healthy cooking techniques, emphasizing organic seasonal produce when possible. Our favorite is the Northwest Eggs Benedict with rosemary-infused hollandaise and smoked wild salmon. (The orange currant scones with lavender-infused syrup are excellent to take along if you go hiking in the Ho Rain Forest in Olympic National Park.)

Every evening (from 4:00-6:00 p.m.) hors d'oeuvres are served along with wines from across Washington State and the Pacific Northwest. We find this is the ideal time to perfect our technique in Colette's most popular on-site activity: the art of relaxation.

Lost Mountain Lodge

Location: Sequim 98382
—on Northeast Olympic Peninsula
Address: 303 Sunny View Drive
Hosts: Dwight & Lisa Hostvedt
Phone: 360.683.2431
Toll Free: 888.683.2431
Email: getaway@lostmountainlodge.com
Web Site: www.lostmountainlodge.com
Rooms: 3 suites & 4 private cottages/ guest houses
Rates: $185–$895
Remarks: "Regardless of where you stay — Main Lodge or one of the cottages- there are expansive views into the snow-capped peaks of the Olympic Mountains."

Secluded in the sunny meadows of i namesake mountain, Lost Mountai Lodge is a Northwest style getaway a surprisingly short drive from lave farms, Olympic National Park and b walks at Dungeness Spit. Large pon a waterfall and natural creek attract wildlife to the Lodge, including balc eagles, blue heron, bobcats and blac tail deer. Its location is inviting for a weekend on the Olympic Peninsula

Owners Dwight and Lisa truly appreciate the outdoors—they sper their honeymoon on a sailboat! An adventurer, Dwight is an award-wir designer craftsman whose work has appeared in magazines. Originally f the East Coast, Lisa has worked for Microsoft, Nordstrom and her own marketing firm. She happily left corporate life behind with the birth of their son, who is the inn's official "cartographer," helping guests put pins in their world map.

Naturally Calm

The bright, airy and artfully simple interiors of the Lodge mirror the colors of the surrounding landscape. Common rooms blend artisan furniture pieces in exotic woods with down-filled, pale cream sofas and chairs. Original artwork and sculpture create a serene and relaxing environment.

The great room has 27-foot vaulted ceilings and an inviting two-story Pennsylvania fieldstone fireplace. We enjoy breakfast al fresco on the deck during summer, taking advantage of the sunny exposure and natural views.

State of Relaxation

The Lost Mountain Lodge offers lavish suites in the Lodge and several large, fully equipped cottages. The Lodge offers uncluttered, Zen-like interiors and furnishings, as well as a dual-waterfall hydrotherapy spa. Three suites provide comfortable king beds with European duvets, hand-pressed linens and contemporary en suite baths. With deep soaking tubs and steam shower rooms, it's tempting to never leave. Weekend packages include hot stone and aromatherapy massage by the wood-burning fireplace in your suite.

Cottages include the two-bedroom Guest House, three-bedroom Summer House, and The Hideaway on Quail Lake. The Hideaway is the largest suite and provides a setting for romance. It includes a nursery with crib, changing table and rocker—ideal for new parents—while honeymooners will enjoy its huge fireplace, jetted tub, and French doors opening to a covered loggia.

Families may be interested in the four-bedroom 1916 Farm House, a Craftsman bungalow three miles away from the main property, with dramatic views of farmland and the Olympic Mountains beyond. The building appears on the National Historic Register as the site of the last World War II Aircraft Lookout Tower in the United States.

The Guest House and 1916 Farm House have private six-person spas, and the Summer House has a vaulted great room with gas fireplace and patio. All cottages provide opulent comfort with king beds, fireplaces, gas grills and beautiful views.

A Full Spread

When staying in Lodge rooms, the sumptuous breakfast begins with fresh fruit, breakfast breads, gourmet cereals, yogurts, juice, coffee, tea, mochas and cappuccinos. I enjoy the Dungeness crab and leek quiche, and Mardi's favorite is peach Amaretti, which is baked peaches stuffed with biscotti, nuts and brandy. It's well worth returning in time for hors d'oeuvres between 4 and 6 p.m. The owners use "farm to table" foods and ingredients from organic farmers in the Sequim-Dungeness Valley, so guests appreciate the wonders of the Olympic Peninsula even more.

BJ's Garden Gate

Location: Port Angeles 98362
—on the Northern Olympic Peninsula
Address: 397 Monterra Drive
Hosts: BJ & Frank Paton
Phone: 360.452.2322
Toll Free: 800.880.1332
Email: info@bjgarden.com
Web Site: www.bjgarden.com
Rooms: 4
Rates: $125–$250
Remarks: "There is something blooming in BJ's garden every month of the year."

Mardi enjoys the story about BJ passion for English gardens and how that inspired the B&B owne BJ and Frank Paton, to build thi waterfront Victorian style Bed and Breakfast.

While on a driving trip through Sequim Dungeness Valley (know to pilots as the Blue Hole), on their way to Butchart Gardens in Victoria B.C., they fell in love wit the area's beauty and the notion how the Olympic Mountains kee the rain at bay on this part of the North Olympic Peninsula. For the Paton's there was nothing lef to do but quit their corporate life and build BJ's Garden Gate!

BJ and Frank have also traveled extensively in Europe, staying in bed and breakfasts, visiting castles and touring gardens. The European experience (and learning what B&B travelers' value) was simply in their blood. Mix European charm with southern hospitality and you begin to get the picture of why they listened to their hearts that day. It's a feeling you too will come to know when you visit.

Built with a B&B in Mind

All guest rooms have oversized picture windows giving a panoramic view of the ocean and gardens. There are four guest suites and all are furnished with period European antiques representing the rulers for which each room is named.

Victoria's Repose, named after Queen Victoria, has a unique English Oak canopy bed and a private porch with a two person hot tub. Napoleon's Retreat enjoys a view of the San Juan Islands, while Marie Antoinette's Boudoir, and Ludwig's Chamber enjoy a view of Victoria Harbor. All four guest suites have a private oversized bath, fireplace (with remote control) and Jacuzzi spa for two.

English Gardens

The B&B is surrounded by two and one-half acres of English gardens and woodland gardens with towering western red cedars and hundreds of rhododendrons. Starting with an empty lot, BJ and Frank have created exceptional gardens—they were recently featured in Country Gardens magazine with an eight page spread featuring the unique collection of plants including BJ's favorite Himalayan blue poppy. Plus, the back gardens overlook nautical miles of blue water leading into the harbor of Victoria in British Columbia.

Mardi's favorite vantage point is from the swing on the large front porch (framed by hanging flower baskets) that looks toward the snow-capped Olympic Mountains. More than once we've spotted whales and often see eagles surfing the air currents overhead while sitting in the back garden overlooking the ocean. Come evening, romantic sunsets are an everyday affair.

Breakfast with a View

You will enjoy a panoramic ocean views from the dining room window as you enjoy BJ's creative traditional breakfast. Mardi's favorite is their baked French stuffed toast made with fresh-picked raspberries from the Sequim Dungeness Valley Farms. I heartily agree, although the chocolate chip cookies served each evening are every bit as delicious.

LOCATION: PORT TOWNSEND 98368
ADDRESS: 1238 WASHINGTON STREET
HOST: CAROL MCGOUGH
PHONE: 360.385.1238
TOLL FREE: 800.385.1238
EMAIL: INFO@JAMESHOUSE.COM
WEB SITE: WWW.JAMESHOUSE.COM
ROOMS: 12
RATES: $145–$250
REMARKS: "OUR FAVORITE MEMORY IS SITTING ON THE GRASSY FRONT LAWN OF THE HILL TOP JAMES HOUSE WHILE WATCHING THE GREEN AND WHITE FERRY DOCKING BELOW IN PORT TOWNSEND."

Built in 1889, the James House is
of Port Townsend's grandest histo
homes and has the distinction of
being the first bed and breakfast i
Pacific Northwest. An exquisite Qu
Anne style mansion (it's included
on the National Register of Histori
Places), it was built on the bluff to
take advantage of the sweeping vie
overlooking Puget Sound and the
snow-capped Olympic Mountains.

YESTERDAY'S ELEGANCE RENEWED

Owned by Carol McGough since 1
this former hospital administrator
turned hotelier also purchased anc
remodeled the adjacent property ir
a Bungalow and Hideaway on the

Bluff in 1996. These two suites both have beautiful water and mountain views, and each have a private garden entry and sitting area.

The ten rooms located in the main house all have private baths, queen beds, and are furnished with elegant antique furniture. Most have water and mountain views and yours may also come with a balcony with private garden views. Request a room in the front and you'll be treated with unobstructed expansive water views with breathtaking mountain vistas to match (our favorites are the Master Suite and the Mt. Rainier Suite).

Common areas for guests to relax with a book or for intimate conversation include the library and formal parlor. On stormy days, the roaring fireplace surrounded by Victorian antiques, comfortable armchairs and couches, plus beautiful oil paintings on the walls creates a private escape that harkens back to the days long before the ferries made regular scheduled runs to the mainland.

The Comforts of Homemade Cuisine

Complimentary sherry is served as an evening aperitif (and you may bring your own alcohol). The homemade cookies (baked daily) add to the warmth of this gracious mansion, but even better is to wake up and smell the delicious aromas of breakfast wafting up the stairs.

Trained at Vermont Culinary Institute, the James House chef prepares a complimentary full hot breakfast served in the formal dining room. Made with herbs grown on the premises, and fresh Northwest seasonal ingredients when possible, it is a hearty affair served with coffee or your favorite tea.

Explore the Gardens & Beyond

Outside, the James House is surrounded by beautiful perennial gardens from early spring until late fall. A picturesque place to relax with an afternoon beverage, Mardi and I find watching the comings and goings of the ferries after a busy day of antiquing through this waterfront town to be the quintessential romantic getaway memory.

Centrally located within the national historic district, the property is within walking distance of all the attractions of Port Townsend. A fitting start would be the historic walking tour through the uptown area (ask to borrow a copy of a walking guide at the front desk).

Nearby, Fort Worden State Park offers trails for hiking, bunkers for exploring, beaches for strolling and beachcombing plus incredible picturing taking opportunities as the sun sets down by the lighthouse. And too, if your visit happens in the summer, check out the concerts at the park in McCurdy Pavilion.

Back in town, Mardi and I enjoy renting a kayak and exploring the Port Townsend waterfront. On foot, there's gallery hopping, book browsing and many coffee shops with outside tables for

LOCATION: PORT TOWNSEND 98368
ADDRESS: 714 WASHINGTON STREET
HOSTS: JOE FINNIE & CINDY FINNIE
PHONE: 360.385.6122
TOLL FREE: 800.824.4738
EMAIL: INFO@RAINSHADOWPROPERTIES.COM
WEB SITE: WWW.BISHOPVICTORIAN.COM
ROOMS: 16 ONE AND TWO BEDROOM SUITES
RATES: $105–$225
REMARKS: "THIS TASTEFULLY RESTORED BRICK BUILDING PLACES YOU AT CENTER-STAGE FOR ALL THAT PORT TOWNSEND HAS TO OFFER."

On the Olympic Peninsula you' find a small Victorian hotel in the heart of one of the most historic towns in Washington. A souvenir of a by-gone era, the Bishop Victorian Hotel is locate in the Bishop Building, a classic four-story brick structure founc in Port Townsend's downtown historic business district. The location is central to everything there is to see in Port Townsenc Admiralty Inlet from Juan de Fuca Straits is one block from the front door of the hotel, and the shops, restaurants, galleries and museums of Port Townsenc are all within a pleasant two blocks' stroll.

Exploring the town is only one of the many things to do in the area. Many guests find the hotel is the perfect place to stay while enjoying water activities such as sailing, kayaking, rowing, and fishing, all available from the nearby Wooden Boat Foundation and vendors.

A Good Game

Hosts Cindy and Joe bring a genuine love of the area and are happy to provide guests with directions and suggestions for getting to know this unique corner of the Olympic Peninsula. A guest doesn't need to leave the hotel to begin exploring the area: Cindy's passion is interior design and art, and her creative vision can be found in the local artwork found throughout the hotel. Joe is an avid golfer and can be talked into a game by his guests. You may frequently find both of your friendly hosts in front of the lobby area fireplace during the hotel's afternoon wine receptions.

Built to Last

The building is an impressive example of the architecture of its time. The façade is Port Townsend brick, and was completed in 1890. All the suites and common rooms are decorated to complement the building's turn-of-the-century style. Each of the sixteen fireplace suites includes one or more bedrooms, private baths, sitting rooms, mini-kitchenettes, and convertible couches that double as beds. Some suites also feature relaxation-inducing soaking tubs.

The "west country English Victorian" décor is consistent throughout the hotel and features antique sideboards, armoires and lighting fixtures in all rooms. Most of the windows of sitting rooms and bedrooms offer attractive views of one kind or another: some offer partial water views, other rooms offer cityscapes or views of the historic buildings, and still others overlooking the hotel's very own spectacular Victorian gardens.

Green and Gold

Cindy assures me that for her the most romantic areas of the hotel unquestionably are the Victorian Gardens—particularly when dressed out and hosting a wedding or reception. The Bishop's award-winning gardens are a short stroll down a staircase behind the hotel. A naturally elegant setting, the gardens are popular among brides, though with a winding path and shaded benches, they're just as well suited for practicing the art of doing nothing after a pleasant afternoon taking a historic tour of nearby Fort Worden.

Impeccable Taste

For breakfasts, guests receive at their door a basket filled with an expansive continental breakfast featuring homemade croissants and scones. Slathering them with butter, it's enough to remind us of days gone by, where the pace was a little slower, style was more refined, service was paramount.

Inn at Port Hadlock

Location: Port Hadlock 98339
Address: 310 Hadlock Bay Road
Host: Debi Bainbridge—General Manager
Phone: 360.385.7030
Toll Free: 800.785.7030
Email: dbainbridge@innatporthadlock.com
Web Site: www.innatporthadlock.com
Rooms: 47 suites and guestrooms
Rates: $99–$349
Remarks: "The views from our elevated bed, over the marina, and beyond to Port Townsend Bay were stunning."

Poised on the south end of Port Townsend Bay, the Inn at Port Hadlock offers a romantic getaway or energizing retreat in one of the most beautiful natural wilderness areas of the Northwest.

Considered to be at the Gateway of the Olympic Peninsula, the inn is situated in a breathtaking alcove, steps away from a 160-slip marina. After recent extensive renovations, under the vision of owner and philanthropist Paul Christiansen, this historic inn surrounds guests with luxury and a high level of service, while preserving the heritage of the Coastal Salish tribes

Rich in Cultural and Economic History

The inn's lands were once a renowned gathering point of the Coastal Salish tribal communities. Over the years, this area transformed into a saw mill (which closed in 1907) and, under the driving force of Charles Adams (Ansel Adam's father), it became an alcohol plant. Abandoned from 1913 until 1978, retired Bellevue Buick dealer Ray Hanson purchased the property and spent $4 million dollars to turn the shell of the saw mill into a beautiful resort. In 2004, the alcohol plant was transformed into the Inn at Port Hadlock.

Hip Meets Luxury and Romance

The inn has 46 extraordinary guest rooms and suites with contemporary Northwest décor. All include a microwave and refrigerator. While each guest room offers a relaxing experience, the rooms overlooking the bay and marina offer spectacular views of Port Townsend Bay, the marina, and Skunk Island. Each water view suite features a fireplace, while Standard and Executive Suites also offer large whirl-jet tubs.

On a recent stay, Mardi and I enjoyed the Romance package, which includes a guest suite with a fireplace and water view. Upon our arrival we found a bottle of champagne waiting for us in the room, gourmet bite-sized French dessert cakes and one dozen roses. Come the next morning, we were treated to breakfast in Nemo's Restaurant.

Water View Dining

Open for breakfast, lunch, and dinner, the award winning onsite Nemo's Restaurant overlooks Port Townsend Bay. The breakfast menu offers many finely prepared selections, including eggs benedict, Belgium waffles, and made-to-order omelets.

The dinner menu is so extensive (including fish, shellfish, pasta, beef, pork, lamb and poultry) that you could spend two weeks at the inn and never eat the same meal twice. I highly recommend their Salmon Pinwheel. Fresh salmon stuffed with sautéed wild mushrooms, wrapped in bacon and topped with demi glaze and a cilantro pesto is the signature presentation from their executive chef, George Eubanks. Follow it up with their white chocolate raspberry cheesecake and you'll have all the energy you need to take an evening stroll through the marina.

The well-trained servers are attentive, yet the unhurried pace lets you enjoy a leisurely meal so you can talk about your plans for the week—from boating to golfing (two excellent courses are nearby), to enjoying the services of their spa or visiting the onsite art gallery The Art Mine.

Exhibiting compelling works of art by artists of national and regional reputation, The Art Mine is the most respected collection on the Olympic Peninsula. This world class art blended with the history, architectural diversity, and water is what makes the inn so memorable.

Willcox House Country Inn

Location: Seabeck 98380
—on Hood Canal
Address: 2390 Tekiu Road NW
Hosts: Cecilia & Phillip Hughes
Phone: 360.830.4492
Toll Free: 800.725.9477
Web Site: www.willcoxhouse.com
Rooms: 5
Rates: $169–$259
Remarks: "This is one of the only places where you feel as though you have been given "permission" to approach the grounds and to stay in the opulent home. This feeling is reinforced by the personal service provided and the intimate, freshly prepared dinner served in the grand dining room. After a few days at the Willcox House it is hard to go back to reality."

At the end of a private drive, throu
emerald green forests opening to
oyster-laden beaches, this waterfrc
mansion is surrounded by an air o
mystery and romance. Commissio
by Colonel Julian P. Willcox in 193
to architect Lionel H. Pries, the
Colonel and his wife Constance liv
here for 30 years. Walking through
the magnificent home, room by ro
you can well imagine the privilege
life this couple shared.

Today, the Willcox House is run by
Phillip and Cecilia Hughes. It is a r
jewel indeed. The fifth owners of t
mansion, they escaped their city jo
to renovate this bed and breakfa

on Hood Canal. Designed in the Beau-Arts tradition, the rooms offer an excursion into an elegance of days long ago.

The library offers views of the Olympic Mountains, a roaring fire, and walls of books. The Great Room has three seating areas, a piano, and the warmth of the immense fireplace. The Game Room with its pool table (and another fireplace) is popular after dinner. There is a Pub Room for socializing and a Movie Theater with a large screen television. The traditional décor is accented with antiques and collectibles.

Let Us Show You to Your Room

All five rooms have a spectacular view of Hood Canal and the Olympic Mountains. There are four double rooms (with king beds) and the fifth room sleeps three. All have a private bath. Constance's room, the most spacious, offers a fireplace. Julian's room, with English country gentleman's décor, features a double Jacuzzi tub. But, Mardi and I favor the Clark Gable room (yes, he was a guest here) with its private balcony overlooking the water and the mountains.

A Private Table for Two and a View

Always make certain to include a dinner with your stay. Served at your own table in the dining room, dinners are romantic with water views and alpenglow sunsets over the Olympics. The regional cuisine has international touches and the wine list (over 100 selections) is outstanding.

Alder roasted wild salmon and crab cakes are house specialties. The on-site herb garden adds delicious flavor and the flower salads are a tasty change. For dessert, chocolate rules, with chocolate truffle cake and chocolate creme brulee (and Mardi has a fond liking for their champagne gelee).

A complimentary complete breakfast is served each morning in the dining room at your own table, which affords you the privacy to talk about your day's activities. Three golf courses are nearby, as are Elandan Bonsai Garden and the 150-acre Bloedel Reserve. Antiquing opportunities abound in the waterfront villages of Poulsbo, Port Townsend and Port Gamble.

There's hiking at Green Mountain and kayaking in Liberty Bay (Poulsbo). Museum buffs have three maritime choices while the Suquamish Native Indian Museum gives insight into the region's rich cultural roots.

Bainbridge Island winery tours are an excellent option…or better yet, simply stay put and relax on the warm swimming beaches just steps from your room. Come the five o'clock hour, socializing with guests over complimentary wine and cheese is enjoyable, as is greeting the new guests arriving by float plane or yacht to the inn's private deep water dock.

Selah Inn on Hood Canal

Location: Belfair 98528
—on Hood Canal
Address: 130 NE Dulalip Landing
Hosts: Bonnie & Pat McCullough
Phone: 360.275.0916
Toll Free: 877.232.7941
Email: innkeeper@selahinn.com
Web Site: www.selahinn.com
Rooms: 7 rooms & a 2 two-bedroom cottage
Rates: $95–$210
Remarks: "For our first visit, we were tipped off to make arrangements for dinner in the inn- was that ever a wise decision! Now it is part of the tradition of enjoying another aspect of Bonnie and Pat's hospitality."

The Hebrew word Selah means "to b at peace, to pause, to meditate." The Indian meaning of Selah is "place o smooth, still waters." Both are just t right words to describe the Selah In a plush bed and breakfast located o the Hood Canal and whose beachfr was once a fishing and gathering pl for local tribes. Many a meal of crab oysters, clams and salmon was shar and many "talk stories" exchanged the shores. The inn is situated off th highway and surrounded by tall fir trees. Local wildlife includes eagles, abundant birds, raccoons, coyotes, deer and sea lions.

Hosts Pat and Bonnie create a warm and friendly atmosphere at the

Selah Inn. Pat is an environmental civil engineer and has worked on projects to help restore salmon runs, estuaries, and water purification in many areas. Bonnie, a former associate pastor, uses her talents and training in foods to the inn's kitchen, creating many delights for breakfast, lunch and dinner. Pat and Bonnie met in college and have been married 43 years, with four children and eleven grandchildren.

The Inn was designed and built in 1997 with the goal of providing guests with superior hospitality and comfort in a beautiful, peaceful setting. The owners have owned adjacent waterfront for 28 years, now living there full-time and are pleased to have the opportunity to share the beauty and peace of Hood Canal with their guests.

Warmth Inside

Through its attractive cedar shakes, broad porch and dormer windows, the Northwest lodge style inn harmonizes well with its natural surroundings The common areas are a continuation of this classic elegance and comfortable flair—especially the library. It's a wonderfully quiet place to curl up with a good book from the bookshelves. In the living room, Mardi and I like to enjoy a glass of wine in front of the river rock fireplace. But, the day starts best in the beautifully tiled sunroom. Wrapped in large windows, it is the setting for the hearty breakfast.

The inn has seven guest rooms with private bathrooms, plus two two-bedroom cottages that share a bathroom. Beds are comfortable kings and queens, and the contemporary style distinguishes all accommodations. Our two favorite rooms—the King Suite and Beach Suite—include private decks with outstanding water views, as well as cozy fireplaces and Jacuzzi tubs.

Northwest Delicacies

A full breakfast is an essential component of a stay at Selah Inn. It includes local fresh fruits and vegetables, apples from the owners' very own orchard, blackberries and huckleberries season, and homegrown herbs.

Be sure to reserve in advance your seats at one of the inn's special five-course dinners. The meal features excellent Northwest seafood, such as fresh halibut, salmon, Dungeness crab, clams, and oysters. Dinner is served in front of the large windows of the sunroom.

Bonnie describes the inn's philosophy well: "My hope is to share the best we have with our guests. That includes the location, the guestrooms and facilities, the food, service and atmosphere. We are here to serve, and we are gratified when our guests' experience becomes a great memory." They succeed in doing just that.

LOCATION: TACOMA 98403
ADDRESS: 705 NORTH 5TH STREET
HOSTS: AARON & KRISTY HOUSE
PHONE: 253.572.1157
TOLL FREE: 888.572.1157
EMAIL: INNKEEPER@VILLABB.COM
WEB SITE: WWW.VILLABB.COM
ROOMS: 5
RATES: $135–$235
REMARKS: "DESIGNED AS A MANSION FOR THE WEALTHY, THIS IMPRESSIVE HOME HAS CHANGED WITH THE TIMES AND APPEARS TO RELISH ITS NEW ROLE AS AN INN WHERE HOSPITALITY IS PROVIDED TO TRAVELERS FROM AROUND THE WORLD."

An historic mansion modeled after an Italian estate, The Villa is an elegant and welcoming bed and breakfast set in the Stadium Distri of Tacoma. With views of the Olympics and Puget Sound, it offer a standout location for exploring the city, as well as warm service an comfort worthy of Italian royalty.

SPECIAL HISTORY

Built in 1925 for the McCormack family, the Villa was designed by A.J. Russell, who also designed the Washington State governor's mans This Italian Renaissance style mansion served as a single-family residence until 1994, when it was converted into a bed and breakfast.

For 12 years Aaron and Kristy lived a few blocks away from The Villa until they purchased it in 2005. Kristy has lived in Tacoma since 1972 and enjoys helping guests get to know the city. She especially loves to cook, while husband Aaron is an avid gardener. A native of eastern Oregon, he has lived in Tacoma for the last eighteen years.

Stroll Through History

Appearing on the National Register of Historic Bed and Breakfasts, The Villa sits on a half-acre lot with extensive gardens and lush flowers that bloom all summer long. The mansion uses warm colors throughout to bring a convivial atmosphere, while antiques complement the classic architecture.

Antique collectors will take note of the 650-year-old mother of pearl inlay Asian chest in the entry area and the 1920 grand piano in living room. Also found in The Villa is a Waterford window that was wrapped in brown paper and brought from Ireland by steamship by Mr. McCormack. The living room is decorated with art glass—fitting for an accommodation located within miles of the Museum of Glass—and a garden room with arched windows.

Italian Style

The Villa's five rooms are decorated with an eclectic mix of antiques and hand-made furniture from the prior owner. One of my favorite rooms is the large, three-room suite "Cimbrone," which has a veranda overlooking a sunken garden and peek-a-boo water and mountain views. In the sitting room, guests may absorb the warmth of the marble-tiled gas fireplace from a love seat that can be also made into a single bed if needed. The oversize tiled shower makes for a refreshing morning—and for evening, the antique soaking tub is big enough for two.

The large king bedroom "Sorrento" has a fireplace and private deck with views of the Olympic Mountains and Puget Sound. All other rooms have queen beds and private baths. The "Amalfi" has a one-person Jacuzzi tub, while the "Caserta" offers a two-person Jacuzzi tub, gas fireplace and the warm sounds of a fountain burbling outside.

The Taste of Tradition

The light-filled dining room where breakfast is served features a hand-made table with seating for fourteen. Breakfast begins with fresh fruit and a scone, and follows with wonderful foods such as eggs Benedict, frittatas, omelets, pancakes and sausage with scrambled eggs. The menu often includes seasonal herbs and other fresh ingredients, and Kristy points out that many guests feel so comfortable that they come to breakfast in their robes. Such is the friendly atmosphere found in the midst of the elegance of The Villa.

Inn at El Gaucho

Location: Seattle 98121
—in Belltown district
Address: 2505 1st Avenue
Host: Teresa Osmena
Phone: 206.728.1133
Toll Free: 866.354.2824
Email: tosmena@elgaucho.com
Web Site: www.inn.elgaucho.com
Rooms: 18 suites
Rates: $155–$345
Remarks: "Without a doubt this was the best room service ever- a sizzling perfectly-prepared steak arriving at my room almost before I finished ordering."

Residing above the renowned El Gaucho steakhouse in the Bellto district of Seattle, The Inn at El Gau is the Emerald City's newest luxury urban inn. With its "retro-swank" f décor and personal pampering, the is an oasis of luxurious indulgence.

Whether it's your first or twenty-fi stay, you'll be treated to the person attention that comes with being a g of Paul Mackay, a legend in Seattle hospitality. Just minutes away fron the Pike Place Market and the Spac Needle, the inn puts you in the cen of all the city has to offer, from shopping and museums, to theater and cultural attractions, plus the m sports venues.

Retro-Swank Fifties Meets Upscale Conveniences

The 18 junior luxury suites are decorated with handmade furnishings, in the same "retro-swank" fifties style synonymous with the El Gaucho name. You'll find Anichini linens, bathrobes, slippers and pajamas plus L'Occitane and Philip B products for hair and body.

While the inn is reminiscent of an earlier era where uncompromising service reigned, is it not lacking in modern amenities. With plasma screen TV with full high-definition digital cable, Bose Wave music system and high speed Internet (both wired and wireless), your room offers you the ultimate in conveniences.

The pillow top queen beds are dressed in fine Anichini linens made with 100% Egyptian cotton and covered with Pacific Coast Feather Co. featherbeds and comforters. No extravagance is spared in the bath as well with Anichini 100% Egyptian oversized cotton towels and bathtubs or showers fitted with The Rain System showerhead.

Some suites offer views over the Atrium, or the city lights and bustling energy of Belltown. Others have sweeping views of Elliott Bay, Olympic Mountains and Puget Sound. And of course, all offer room service from the inn's namesake restaurant, the incomparable El Gaucho.

Uncompromising Service

The inn's 24-hour concierge service is available to assist you with procuring tickets, town car service, and other arrangements to help you fully enjoy your stay. Mardi and I were especially pleased to see the inn partner with premier merchants including gym and health club services at the Seattle Athletic Club and spa services.

The inn's main lobby has a welcoming fireplace which offers private seating for quiet conversations. Our favorite spot, however, is the intimate piano bar at El Gaucho Restaurant. What could be more romantic than making a request for your special song and have it dedicated to the one you love?

While the dining room offers excellent service in a hip atmosphere, I highly recommend you request the in-room dining "bedside" preparation provided by El Gaucho steakhouse. Available until midnight (until 10 p.m. on Sunday), it is an affordable indulgence far from the ordinary.

Surprise Her with a Romance Package

When the occasion calls for something just a tad bit more special, such as an anniversary or birthday, the Inn at El Gaucho offers a Romance Package that turns the day into a heartfelt event. In addition to your junior suite for the night, you also receive fresh flowers, Billecart Salmon champagne served in your room, chocolate truffles, plus a $100 dining credit to El Gaucho with priority reservations and seating. It's an experience that you'll both remember forever.

THE SORRENTO HOTEL

LOCATION: SEATTLE 98104
ADDRESS: 900 MADISON
HOST: DELLA-RAE CARRIERE
PHONE: 206.622.6400
TOLL FREE: 800.426.1265
EMAIL: RESERVATIONS@HOTELSORRENTO.COM
WEB SITE: WWW.HOTELSORRENTO.COM
ROOMS: 76 GUESTROOMS AND SUITES
RATES: $305–525
REMARKS: "ONCE A YEAR MARDI AND I SNEAK OFF TO EXPERIENCE SEATTLE AS VISITORS. OUR STAY ALWAYS INCLUDES AN INDULGENT DINNER AT THE HUNT CLUB AND A PAMPERED OVERNIGHT STAY AT THE SORRENTO."

A striking combination of beauty ar history is found in Seattle's notable Sorrento Hotel. Located in downtow on First Hill, the hotel is a central point for exploring Seattle icons such as the Space Needle and Pike Place Market. The Sorrento provides sophisticated accommodations within a historic city landmark—an excellent service to match.

AN ICON OF SEATTLE

The Sorrento was built in 1909 and showcases the talents of architect Harlan Thomas, whose design was inspired by a visit to Sorrento, Italy. Reflecting this classic style today is the hotel's Fireside Room, with its dark wooden paneling and comfortable furniture. Guests may appreciate this décor during afternoon tea, served every day with a full selection of teas, finger sandwiches, sweets and the requisite scones with Devonshire cream. If you're too late for tea, it's also a fine spot to have a drink before dinner.

The original owner of the Sorrento Hotel, Samuel Rosenberg, was a pioneer and Seattle clothing merchant who decided to try his hand at running a luxury hotel. The hotel's opening coincided with the Alaska Yukon Pacific Exposition, during which the Sorrento was visited by some of the most celebrated members of early twentieth century society. In fact, the hotel's first registered guest was none other than President William Taft.

In December 1981, new owner and music industry executive Michael Malone reopened the seven-story hotel after an extensive restoration. The new design included more space for guests by converting the original 150 guest rooms into just 76 rooms, many of which are now suites with separate seating areas.

Meeting High Expectations

The Sorrento's rooms have a timeless and elegant decor, including embroidered decorative pillows, but with all the modern essentials. Deluxe rooms have king or queen beds (a few have two queens) with well-appointed Italian marble bathrooms. Rooms also include a French press coffee service that goes well with the morning newspaper.

The Sorrento's most impressive accommodation—one fit for a celebratory occasion—is the 1,850 square foot Penthouse Suite. Its elegant master bedroom features a king bed covered in 400 thread-count Egyptian cotton linens and the pillow of your choice, selected from the pillow menu. The highlight of the Italian marble bathroom is the two-person "fill from the ceiling" jetted tub. After a relaxing and dramatic bath, there's no better place to appreciate the Seattle skyline than the suite's outdoor terrace. Or if it happens to be raining, tickle the ivories on the suite's baby grand piano while your significant other basks in the light of the wood-burning fireplace.

Full of Taste

Sorrento's established fine restaurant is The Hunt Club, which serves a full repertoire of Northwest foods created with a Mediterranean touch. Ingredients are selected from in-season, local and artisan-farmed products, including many organic ingredients. The menu changes seasonally, and we particularly enjoy the rack of lamb with minted pea ravioli and a heady rosemary jus. With arched windows and mahogany walls, the dining room is one of the most romantic areas of the hotel. It provides exceptional service, as one might have expected during the turn of the previous century.

LOCATION: SEATTLE 98119 —7-DAY CRUISE DEPARTS PIER 30
ADDRESS: 300 ELLIOTT AVENUE WEST
CORPORATE OFFICES: 206.281.3535
TOLL FREE: 800.426.0327
WEB SITE: WWW.HOLLANDAMERICA.COM
ROOMS: VARY BY SHIP, FROM 1150 SQ FT PENTHOUSE, TO 160-190 SQ FT OCEANVIEW AND INSIDE STATEROOMS.
RATES: RATES VARY BY SHIP AND DEPARTURE DATES
REMARKS: "WE HAVE FOUND THIS CRUISE TO BE THE PERFECT VACATION FOR OUR CHILDREN AND PARENTS, MAKING IT EASY TO HAVE FAMILY TIME TOGETHER, ALL THE WHILE ENJOYING THE PASSING SCENERY, GLACIERS AND THIS INCREDIBLE MARINE COASTLINE."

While this selection may seem a odd in a book of top places to stay in Washington, a Holland Americ cruise to Alaska is a wonderful option for a relaxing week.

Leaving from Seattle, it offers the best of all worlds: the privacy of y stateroom, delectable internation cuisine, non-stop activities, a heal club, plus a warm and gracious service staff. And you haven't eve left the dock yet!

Sailing along Alaska's Inside Pass you'll marvel at towering glaciers, cascading waterfalls, and forests hung in mists as you cruise to stunning Glacier Bay National Pa or the mammoth Hubbard Glacie in Wrangell-St. Elias National Park. Every port is a new adventure—from the rugged beauty of Juneau, Sitka, and Ketchikan to the sophistication of Victoria. There is a comprehensive program of excursions available in every port, so you can tailor your Alaskan experience.

Known for a classical cruising style, Holland America caters to those who prefer elegant surroundings with a quiet serenity. Onboard, Mardi and I found like-minded couples looking for a new travel experience rather than singles looking to meet other singles.

From Inside Cabin to Penthouse Suite

A hallmark of Holland America is they have larger staterooms than most mass-market cruise lines—whether you choose a standard inside cabin, outside stateroom, standard balcony cabin or Penthouse Suite.

We chose a standard balcony cabin with a spacious veranda. It had the ambiance of a fine European hotel complete with a pillow-top bed, a duvet and high-thread count sheets, plus the stocked mini-bar, and two thick bath robes. The fresh flowers and fresh fruit bowl were a special touch.

Throughout the ship were antiques and reproductions, much use of marble and luxurious fabrics. The open promenade deck featured the line's signature teak and cushioned deck loungers—quite the classic touch!

Varied Venues and Many Menus

Breakfast and lunch are fabulous buffets and there are several dining rooms. You'll find your favorite choices—from Italian and Asian to a deli custom sandwich, plus tacos, grilled hamburgers and hot dogs. As Seattle is Holland America's home city, there is an entire restaurant devoted to Northwest specialties. Their Grand Marnier Chocolate Volcano Cake is a dessert you must share with your partner at least once during your voyage!

Dinner is a special affair with three to four seating times at tables for two, four, six, and eight. A dramatic two-story dining room with floor-to-ceiling windows offers breathtaking sea views. China, sparkling crystal, and crisp linens are the norm. Twenty-four hour room service is always an option as well—whether you want to snack in between meals or order directly off the dinner menu.

Poolside is Only the Beginning

It is tempting to fill up your time with activities, like the Culinary Arts classes or spa treatments-don't! Relaxing has its own reward. We found nothing could compare with a walk topside after dark. Without the interference of city lights, the sky simply comes alive with the twinkling of stars. And, if you've never seen a glacier by the glow of moonlight, it is truly something to behold.

LOCATION: BELLEVUE 98004
ADDRESS: 11200 SOUTHEAST 6TH STREET
HOSTS: JONATHAN BARTLETT—HOTEL MANAGER; LENELLA TABOR—DIRECTOR OF SALES & MARKETING
PHONE: 425.454.4424
TOLL FREE: 800.579.1110
EMAIL: HOTEL@BELLEVUECLUB.COM
WEB SITE: WWW.BELLEVUECLUBHOTEL.COM
ROOMS: 67 TOTAL—19 DELUXE GUESTROOMS; 34 PREMIER GUESTROOMS; 11 CLUB GUESTROOMS; 1 FOUNTAIN SUITE; 1 WILBURTON SUITE; 1 RAINIER SUITE
RATES: $205–$1,500
REMARKS: "THIS IS WASHINGTON'S ANSWER TO THE CHALLENGE OF HOW TO ENJOY WORLD-CLASS ACCOMMODATIONS AND FINE FOOD WITHOUT GAINING WEIGHT—ATTACH THE HOTEL TO A STATE-OF-THE-ART ATHLETIC CLUB AND GIVE THE GUESTS FULL PRIVILEGES."

Casually elegant, the Bellevue Club Hotel is a private retreat in the mid of a dynamic city setting. Surround by lush green gardens, this four-diamond, award-winning boutique hotel offers guests a quiet urban ha with easy access to a broad array of Bellevue shopping district, downto Seattle, as well as the skiing, golfin and hiking in the nearby Cascades.

A HISTORY OF SERVICE

The Bellevue Club opened its doors 1979 with the mission to be a socia and athletic facility. Two and a half decades later, the Club is known as place for wellness, recreation and hospitality. Over the years the Club grew dramatically and made many enhancements, including opening the luxurious 67-room hotel in 1994.

Luxury with a View

All of the hotel's guest rooms and suites include special touches such as goose down pillows and feather duvets. The marble, limestone, and granite bathrooms encourage guests to linger in the glass-enclosed shower with Mardi's favorite Molton Brown bath products.

The most romantic room of the hotel is undoubtedly the Rainier Suite. Perfect for a very special getaway, the room has a fireplace, jetted tub and two balconies with breath-taking views of Mount Rainier. This suite's décor includes an imported Tupelo wood floor and Persian rugs. With a formal living area complete with fireplace, dining room table for eight to twelve guests, a wet bar, and two balconies the word to describe this suite is sumptuous.

The bedroom is separated from the living room by frosted glass pocket doors and features a stunning master bath with an oversized double glass enclosed shower and steps leading to a sunken, jetted tub.

Indulge Your Athletic Side

Under the same roof as the hotel, the club's facilities are open to non-members who stay at the hotel as well as its regular members. Mardi and I enjoy the club's indoor Olympic-sized swimming pool and hot tub during our stays, but there are also indoor and outdoor tennis courts, racquetball and squash courts, a gymnasium and indoor running track, two restaurants, four fitness studios, a grand ballroom, a childcare center and a boutique shop.

After a refreshing afternoon swim, the Terrace Room is the place to recharge and enjoy the complimentary tea. The relaxed living room is open to guests and has comfortable seating in front of the fireplace. There you'll also find coffee service in the morning to get you headed out the door for your next adventure.

Relaxing Delights

With room service available 24 hours, Mardi and I indulge ourselves with the decadence of dinner in our own room. The food is exceptionally good under the direction of Executive Chef Paul Marks. Mardi especially enjoys the flavorful curried halibut, while I dig into the herb-crusted lamb rack. Wrapped in our thick bathrobes, we find there's no better way to enjoy the view from our room than working through the extraordinary flourless chocolate cake with a raspberry rosemary coulis. After a day filled with sights and athletics, it's just the thing to nourish the body—and the soul.

SALISH LODGE & SPA

LOCATION: SNOQUALMIE 98065
ADDRESS: 6501 RAILROAD AVENUE SE
HOST: SAM JOHNSON—GENERAL MANAGER
PHONE: 425.888.2556
TOLL FREE: 800.2.SALISH
EMAIL: RESERVATIONS@SALISHLODGE.COM
WEB SITE: WWW.SALISHLODGE.COM
ROOMS: 89
RATES: $199–$699
REMARKS: "THIS WORLD-CLASS HOTEL HAS IT ALL FIGURED OUT-THEY BLEND MARVELOUS ARCHITECTURE, A BREATHTAKING LOCATION ABOVE A MASSIVE WATERFALL WITH EXCEPTIONAL FOOD, SPA TREATMENTS AND THEN ADD IN A LUXURIOUS ROOM - WHAT MORE COULD YOU ASK FOR?"

Set atop the crest of Snoqualmie Falls—considered by many to be a sacred place—the Salish Lodge & Spa looks over the dramatic 268-foot waterfall and lush forests and mountains beyond.

The Salish Lodge's rustic elegance permeates its Northwest lodge déc with a stone floor entryway and wood accents throughout. The first Lodge was built in 1916 as a food and rest stop to meet the needs of waterfall-seeking tourists. Today, Snoqualmie Falls is one of the mos visited tourist destinations in the state of Washington—and the Sali Lodge is the place to truly apprecia its beauty.

A Classic Lodge

All the lodge's 89 guestrooms feature one king or two double beds and are elegantly decorated with tasteful black and white Snoqualmie Falls photography and custom built furniture. Most of the rooms face the Snoqualmie River, and many have small decks.

The sleek bathrooms feature specially blended Salish toiletries. After soaking away the workweek in the two-person, oversized whirlpool spa baths, the natural place to relax is in front of the room's fireplace. A bedtime chocolate and the feather bed is most welcome with its down pillows and 320 thread-count linens. The gentle sounds of the waterfall wash away any lingering stress.

For those looking for even more relaxation, the spa provides ample indulgence, with an Asian-inspired setting and signature treatments such the heated stone massage and Snoqualmie Falls foot refresher. The eucalyptus steam room, dry sauna, and therapeutic soaking pools are available at any time throughout a spa visit.

Tranquility continues in the lodge library, where a roaring fire, books and board games await. Morning coffee and afternoon tea are available for guests every day.

Notable Culinary Tradition

Dining is an essential experience at the Salish Lodge. Built around the original 1916 fireplace, the dining room combines Northwest character and casual elegance for a special dining experience guided by Executive Chef Roy Breiman. In its renowned restaurant, called simply The Dining Room, guests can feast on the same famous four-course country breakfast that has been the talk of many local towns for generations.

With extensive experience working in Michelin starred restaurants, Chef Roy has traveled the world learning about the foods of diverse cultures and enriching his palate. He brings to the Salish Lodge a powerful combination of culinary traditions from the grand cities of Europe to the bustling streets of Southeast Asia.

Mardi and I like to indulge in the exceptional tableside service—and, of course, the beautiful view; not to mention the largest selection of Northwest wines and their award-winning wine list. Chef Roy's flawless Oregon Country beef chateaubriand comes with a smooth béarnaise sauce, and I can't stay away from their Valrhona chocolate "bombe" with a soft truffle filling. For a more casual meal, the Attic Bistro serves lunch and dinner every day and offers a bird's eye view of the falls, with meals made with the same skill and fresh ingredients as the Dining Room.

Explore the Foothills of the Cascades

Salish Lodge & Spa's location puts many different outdoor activities and excursions within easy reach. A bike, trail, or even a kayak provides sweeping views of beautiful foliage and rocky peaks—all in the serenity of the Snoqualmie Valley.

LOCATION: WOODINVILLE 98072
ADDRESS: 14590 NE 145TH STREET
HOSTS: RON ZIMMERMAN & CARRIE VAN DYCK
PHONE: 425.485.5300
EMAIL: RESERVATIONS@THEHERBFARM.COM
WEB SITE: THEHERBFARM.COM
ROOMS: 2 SUITES
RATES: $250–$395
REMARKS: "THE HERBFARM—WHERE LIFE IS AS PERFECT AS YOU HAD ALWAYS HOPED IT WOULD BE."

Fresh beauty, slow food, and elegan surroundings, The Herbfarm is a pl of sensory indulgence. At the core i its exquisite restaurant, one of the best in the region, if not the countr The Herbfarm's accommodations a an extension of the dining experier allowing guests to spend an idyllic time in the rich embrace of the Sammamish River Valley.

IT STARTED WITH A WHEELBARROW

In 1974, Lola Zimmerman parked a wheelbarrow full of homegrown he at the side a rural road 20 miles fro Seattle. Its sign read "Herb Plants fo Sale," and a Mason honor jar collect the receipts. Encouraged by the first season's sales, Lola and her husband expanded the herb sales, and their little farm grew into the Northwest's largest herb farm over the next ten years.

In 1986, the Zimmerman's son Ron sold his company and joined The Herbfarm, as it was now known. He and his wife, Carrie Van Dyke, remodeled the family's garage and opened it as a country restaurant serving six-course luncheons. The restaurant quickly garnered fame and for the next 10 years played to sold-out houses. Executive chef Jerry Traunfeld came on board in the summer of 1990.

When The Herbfarm was destroyed by fire in 1997, the restaurant moved into a large tent, then a local winery, and finally reopened in its current Woodinville location along with two guest suites. The new restaurant and suites were constructed from hundreds of found and salvaged architectural pieces, many from the early twentieth century. One such piece is found in the Herbfarm salon: a one-of-a-kind 100-year-old sea captain's fireplace.

Farm-Style Tradition

The Herbfarm shares five acres along the Sammamish River with the Willows Lodge. Built in 2000, the Herbfarm's building was inspired by historic architecture in rural Ireland and France. Its décor is comfortably elegant with heavy timbers and rustic touches.

The two large suites are individually decorated with antiques and original art overlooking the herb gardens. They share a magnificent view of Mt. Rainier to the south. Both rooms have private baths. The Orchard House Suite is decorated in upscale French country style, with fabrics purchased in France, original antiques, and artwork. The Herb Garden Suite has an English garden theme expressed through the antiques and original artwork. Both suites feature queen beds with hand-sewn mattresses. They also offer fireplaces and private balconies, both ideal locations to sip a complimentary glass of fine Sherry. Views from rooms are of the large green valley of Woodinville, as well as the inn's namesake herb gardens.

Fresh on the Table

Dinner at the Herbfarm is an experience. The prix fixe nine-course menus change 25 times a year to follow seasonally available foods, and no ingredients are used from outside of the greater Pacific Northwest. The Herbfarm Restaurant grows most of the herbs and vegetables used throughout the year, and it employs a year-round wild food forager. Its menus and desserts are always different—Mardi is still talking about her Oregon black truffle ice cream. Suffice it to say, The Herbfarm never fails in its goal: to make time spent there as perfect as you had always hoped it would be.

Boatyard Inn

Location: Langley 98260 —on Whidbey Island
Address: 200 Wharf Street
Host: Mynda Myres
Phone: 360-221-5120
Email: boatyard@whidbey.com
Web Site: www.boatyardinn.com
Rooms: 10
Rates: $130–$230
Remarks: "This inn is as close to the water as you can get without getting your feet wet."

If you long to fall asleep at night to the sound of waves lapping, or wan to wake to the sight of the sun risir over the snowcapped Cascades and spilling across Saratoga Passage, th the Boatyard Inn is just the place fc the two of you.

Located in Langley Village on Whidbey Island, this traditional Northwest style two-story inn is reminiscent of an old cannery with its corrugated metal roofs, colorful siding and wood columns. But inside, the 1994 structure tells a fa different story.

The ten studio suites, deluxe studios and loft suites are contemporary (think Eddie Bauer™ décor), oversized (from 600 to 1,000 square feet) with every convenience built-in. All have spacious living rooms with gas fireplace, queen bed, private bath, galley kitchen, and a romantic waterfront (or water view) deck. Sitting on the deck is like having front row seats to watching all the action in the shipping lanes of Saratoga Passage and the town's working waterfront.

Location, Location, Location

A stone's throw away you'll find a 30-foot marina, public boat ramp and fishing pier where seagulls circle with their characteristic cry. A short stroll in the other direction takes you into the heart of Langley Village. This haven of boutiques, galleries, and antique shops is full of unique finds, and the restaurants offer truly flavorful cuisine.

Sitting at an outside café table (surrounded by shopping bags), sipping on a glass of wine with the sun on Mardi's face, I can tell you firsthand that an afternoon in this idyllic setting is definitely the way to a woman's heart. And the salt air seems to add to the mix.

Heard it Through the Grapevine

Innkeeper Mynda Myres is a true local who grew up on Whidbey Island. She and her assistant, Faye Elliot, enjoy sharing the secrets of this seahorse-shaped island with you, including the best of what there is to see and do.

Mardi and I enjoy kayaking and beachcombing along the ten miles of sandy beach at Ebey's Landing. You can catch whale watching trips in town, and nearby Deception Pass is a great hiking spot. The local wineries invite you with wine tasting and if you feel adventurous you can rent a tandem bike to take you there.

The Best Time to Visit

While every season offers its own reasons why the Boatyard Inn is a compelling destination, we especially enjoy our mid-winter visits. Regardless of when we do visit, the hospitality of the innkeepers and their willingness to share their little part of the world adds to the total experience. The simple rhythm of the day (beginning with a continental breakfast enjoyed on our private deck) simply works its magic—as does the night.

There is nothing quite so romantic as watching the sight of a full moon rising up over the Cascades from the vantage point of your raised bed. That means twelve visits a year would be in order. (Full moons create wonderful low tides too for excellent beach combing!)

LOCATION: LANGLEY 98260
—ON WHIDBEY ISLAND
ADDRESS: 400 FIRST STREET,
P O BOX 835
HOSTS: MATT COSTELLO—GENERAL MANAGER
PHONE: 360.221.3033
EMAIL: INFO@INNATLANGLEY.COM
WEB SITE: WWW.INNATLANGLEY.COM
ROOMS: 26
RATES: $175–$495
REMARKS: "A WONDERFUL DINNER, FINE WINES AND NO DRIVING MADE THIS OUR ANNIVERSARY CHOICE."

Built into a bluff overlooking Saratc Passage on Whidbey Island, the award-winning Inn at Langley puts you within walking distance to all c all of the art galleries, antique store and boutiques in the waterfront village of Langley. Offering a peacef balance between relaxation and outdoor activities, it's a private have for a romantic getaway close to hom

The inn provides a peaceful, Zen-lik environment. Works of local artists are found in all of the common areas. Guestrooms create a persona sanctuary with the use of space, natural fabrics and rich furnishings a simple setting.

Watch the View and Feel Renewed

Each of the inn's 22 guestrooms, two suites and two cottages feature 180-degree waterfront views and an oversized jetted tub, situated to face the fireplace and the Puget Sound. Large, outdoor porch-style balconies give you a front row seat to beautiful sunrises over the Cascade Mountains on the mainland and romantic sunsets over Saratoga Passage.

More than once Mardi and I have heard the distinctive sound of the gray whales breathing at night in the dark waters beyond our balcony. Even though we couldn't see them as we peered out into the night, we surely knew they were there. These are experiences we will never forget.

The suites are oversized, with a private bedroom and a sitting room with a deck. Even larger are the two-story cottages. Each offers almost 1,000 square feet with a generous living room area on the main floor and a private bedroom on the floor below.

Get Up Close with the Chef

The heart of the inn is the Chef's Kitchen Restaurant. An open display kitchen with a double-sided river rock fireplace, its entrance is through a formal herb garden and fruit trees and opens to a dining room that seats 36. Twelve guests can be seated at the Chef's Table, which is centrally located in front of the kitchen (Mardi and I find this is be the best seat in the house).

Chef/General Manager Matt Costello prepares a six-course dinner on Friday, Saturday and Sunday evenings, adding Thursday nights in the summer. With extensive award-winning credits in the Northwest, his experience includes chef positions at the Four Seasons Olympic Hotel, plus both the Dahlia Lounge and Palace Kitchen, where he joined with the famous Seattle Chef Tom Douglas.

Chef Matt's cuisine is seasonally inspired by the fresh ingredients of Whidbey Island and the region and complemented by selections from the inn's extensive Northwest wine collection. A complimentary Breakfast Buffet is served daily featuring a European-style breakfast including fresh baked pastries, fresh fruit, quiche and frittata, house-made granola, and more.

Three Must-Do Activities

Wildly popular with the guests, be sure to ask about the Chef's Kitchen Cooking Classes available during your stay. Whether or not you consider yourself a gourmet cook, you'll return from your romantic getaway with the culinary skill to impress your friends and family (at least on one dish!). Other must-do adventures during your stay include beachcombing and indulging in your choice of treatments in the onsite Spa Essencia. Complete with three massage rooms, and a steam/wet room, it is an incredible way to soak up the deep peace of the island.

LOCATION: LA CONNER 98257
ADDRESS: 121 MAPLE AVENUE
HOSTS: LORI & STEPHEN FARNELL
PHONE: 360.466.1400
TOLL FREE: 800.477.1400
EMAIL: INFO@WILDIRIS.COM
WEB SITE: WWW.WILDIRIS.COM
ROOMS: 18
RATES: $119–$209
REMARKS: "AFTER 20+ YEARS OF VISITING INNS, I HAVE CONSUMED MY FAIR SHARE OF GREAT COOKIES, BUT I HAVE NEVER EXPERIENCED COOKIES AS GOOD AS THE ONES THE WILD IRIS INN BAKES EACH DAY—THEY EVEN HAD MARDI TRYING TO GET THE RECIPE."

An inn designed to feel like a country manor, Wild Iris Inn presents a picture-perfect place to rest during a full weekend of watching whales in Puget Sound, viewing fields of spring tulips, and shopping and dining in La Conner.

Hosts Steve and Lori became innkeepers thanks to their love of sailing in the waters near La Conn[er]. Lori had been working in sales and marketing in the hotel industry for 25 years, and Steve worked in the food and beverage area of the hotel industry for eight years prior to becoming a lawyer. Their sailing afforded them plenty of opportunities to visit La Conner, and they fell in love with the town's unique character. They soon realized they could use their hotel knowledge and live in a town they truly enjoyed. It took six years to find their ideal inn: the Wild Iris.

Bucolic Setting

Built in 1992, the inn's comfortable lobby area welcomes guests with a large river rock fireplace. Each of the inn's 18 rooms is uniquely decorated—from contemporary to country cottage—and all are specially designed for couples looking for a romantic and quiet getaway. We find the Wild Iris a comfortable blend between the charm of a personally run inn and the amenities and services you would expect to find in an upscale hotel. Most rooms have private porches or balconies with pastoral views of the farmland behind the inn and distant views of the Cascade Mountains. Many varieties of flowers and vegetables are grown on nearby land, yet La Conner's downtown shops are just blocks away.

All but two of the rooms have generous king beds, with comfortable bedding and bed linens, plush towels and robes. Nearly all of the rooms also offer jetted spa tubs and fireplaces, designed to give guests the feeling that they have escaped to their own estate in the country.

With a name like "Wild Iris," it may come as no surprise that fresh flowers await guests every day in their rooms, as well as delicious cookies. The inn also offers special in-room packages that can be ordered in advance: spa baskets, wine and cheese trays, Champagne and chocolates, as well as flower arrangements.

Breakfast for Two

Breakfast is a tasty and generous two-course meal in the dining room. Guests can look forward to homemade granola—one of the house specialties—or fresh homemade pastry each day for the first course, as well as a hearty second course that may include eggs and breakfast meats. The private dining room serves breakfast at intimate tables set for two. Isolation is not required, though; larger groups can be accommodated in the dining room or the inn's meeting room. The innkeepers are happy to bring breakfast to your room, if you let them know ahead of time that you're planning to sleep in.

With so much to do in La Conner and the surrounding area, it may be difficult to make time for relaxation during your weekend. Steve and Lori always make sure that after hiking, kayaking, river rafting, bicycling, boating, whale watching, beachcombing or other activity the Wild Iris provides a quiet place to simply relax and unwind.

Majestic Inn and Spa

Location: Anacortes 98221
Address: 419 Commercial Street
Host: Susie Deyo—General Manager
Phone: 360.299.1400
Toll Free: 877.370.0100
Email: info@majesticinnandspa.com
Web Site: www.majesticinnandspa.com
Rooms: 21
Rates: $129–$329
Remarks: "In addition to Mardi's pilgrimage to the Majestic spa, we both find the inn and restaurant ideal for a stay before and following any ferry trip from Anacortes."

With the hallmark cupola on top, this award-winning establishment Fidalgo Island (accessible by bridge offers guests the romance of an historic inn with the sophisticatior a modern day spa and the fine cuis of an acclaimed restaurant.

Originally known as the Anacortes Mercantile, the building was erecte in 1889 on the corner of 8th and I Street. Later it was placed on rolling logs and pulled by horses to its current location in the historic downtown area. In the fall of 2005 innkeepers Michael Keenan, Bob Moran, and Guy Davidson had the Majestic Inn and Spa remodeled into the elegant inn it is today.

With a complimentary continental breakfast (and a free pass to a local fitness center) plus its nearby surroundings offering gallery walks, antiquing, and island hopping adventures, you'll find the Majestic Inn and Spa a world-class choice in a romantic Northwest destination.

Putting a Facelift on History

With 21 spacious rooms ranging from single to adjoining suites, all have been completely remodeled to offer luxurious comfort with elegantly designed Northwest interiors. All have a private bath with special amenities including luxurious robes, aromatherapy soaps, lotions, and shampoos. Most rooms have wet-bars, some have soaking tubs, and for the ultimate in romance, request a room with a private deck.

For a special occasion (or to turn an ordinary day into a memorable event), make it a point to reserve the Majestic Suite. With a living room, bedroom, two baths (with enormous walk-in shower and double-jetted Jacuzzi for two), two decks and two plasma televisions, this suite will make you feel like royalty.

Rooms of Adventure

The main floor of the inn offers many interesting rooms to explore, including the Fireplace Room and the lively Pub. Two antique glass doors open to a long bar and groupings of inviting chairs and tables. With an extensive wine list, exceptional martini selection and signature cocktails, the Pub is a great gathering place that hosts local and regional entertainers on Friday and Saturday nights.

The on-site luxury Chrysalis Spa and Salon offers massages, facials, body treatments, plus manicures, pedicures, waxing and hair services. Mardi raves about the service and reappears totally rejuvenated. While she is being attended to I drop into their retail Spa Boutique to purchase her favorite lotions to gain points with her on Mother's Day.

Expertly Prepared, Exquisitely Served

Open and airy with floor-to-ceiling windows, Anna's at the Majestic is a stunning dining room with an equally inspired menu. Executive Chef David Burdette presents regional dishes infused with European influences. An inspiring chef with 25 years of fine food experience in 5-star resorts, hotels, and fine dining establishments, David's dynamic personality simply comes through his cuisine. My favorite is his macadamia nut crusted halibut. For a divine dessert, order the apple crumble with seasonal fresh fruit for the two of you to share.

After dinner, Mardi and I enjoy retreating to the cupola atop the inn. This intimate room has a sitting area with windows all around to enjoy the view of Anacortes. If you follow this with a show at the live theatre nearby, you'll find it's a romantic way to end your evening.

LOCATION: FRIDAY HARBOR 98250
—ON SAN JUAN ISLAND
ADDRESS: 235 C STREET
HOSTS: ANNA MARIA DE FREITAS & DAVID PASS—OWNERS, MICHAEL BUCKLEY—INNKEEPER
PHONE: 360.378.3587
TOLL FREE: 800.407.7933
EMAIL: INNKEEPER@HARRISONHOUSESUITES.COM
WEB SITE: WWW.HARRISONHOUSESUITES.COM
ROOMS: 5 SUITES
RATES: $175–375
REMARKS: "THIS HILLSIDE INN IS IDEAL FOR FAMILIES OR FRIENDS AS IT IS VERY CONVENIENT TO TOWN AND DESIGNED WITH PLENTY OF SPACE THAT PROMOTES PRIVACY YET EASY INTERACTIONS AMONG GUESTS."

Enjoying a spectacular view of the town and marina of Friday Harbor, this hilltop retreat in a restored 19(Craftsman-style is just one and hal blocks from the ferry landing in a quiet residential neighborhood. Originally named the Middleton House, it was renamed the Harriso House when it converted to a Bed and Breakfast. Today, the Harrison House Suites Bed & Breakfast consists of two buildings—the historic Middleton House and a second building which houses the 1930 Roche Harbor Cottage and th Garden Café.

The Harrison House is a dream come true for proprietors Dave P and Anna Maria de Freitas, who first saw the Harrison House in August of 2004 during their 5-year quest to find the perfect B&B opportunity. Five months later they moved to Friday Harbor from Maryland as the inn's new owners.

Having spent years traveling the world to many B&Bs, they developed a sixth sense for what guests want most during their stay. What drew them to their life as innkeepers is their love of entertaining and sharing fine cooked meals.

Four Suites and a Cottage

The San Juan is the largest suite (1650 square feet) with three bedrooms and two baths. This vacation "home" with dining room, eat-in kitchen, large family room (with piano) plus a huge private deck has its own barbecue and shared hot tub, with views of the town and harbor.

Lopez Suite is a two bedroom suite that sleeps eight and has a kitchen, bath and living room plus a viewing deck. Shaw Suite is a nautical themed studio suite (sleeps 4) with a kitchen and bath. The 1930 Roche Harbor Cottage (in a separate building) is a one bedroom suite with kitchen, living room, fireplace and deck with private hot tub.

Nicknamed the honeymoon suite (although it can sleep four), the Orcas is the favorite suite of Mardi and mine because of its views of the water, sunrises and sunsets, and outer islands—plus it has its own private hot tub and deck. With fireplace, mini-kitchen, private bath with jetted tub, and tasteful furnishings, this roomy suite is the perfect romantic hideaway.

Dishes from Anna Maria's Own Cookbook

Prior to becoming innkeepers, Anna Maria worked in public broadcasting for 20 years, traveling the world with Dave to food-centric cultures. Her cookbook, La Cucina Anna Maria: Good Life Recipes from San Juan Island, is the result of her culinary experiences and inspires her menu at the B&B today.

Local farmers and fisherman supply fresh seasonal ingredients (including chicken and duck eggs, produce, meats, fish, and cheeses) which are prepared with fruit and herbs from the B&B's own organic garden.

A full four-course complimentary breakfast of the guest's choice is served in the Garden Café (and can be delivered to your room). The Southwest Scramble is my favorite, while Mardi simply craves the lemon ricotta pancakes. For dinner, their local island lamb smoked with an Indonesian marinate flavored with soy and Brazil nuts is excellent. All in all, the food is simply excellent and adds to the old-world hospitality celebrated in this B&B's motto: "Guest come as strangers, leave as friends and return as part of the extended family."

TUCKER HOUSE INN

LOCATION: FRIDAY HARBOR 98250
—ON SAN JUAN ISLAND
ADDRESS: 260 B STREET
HOSTS: ANNA MARIA DE FREITAS & DAVID PASS—OWNERS, MICHAEL BUCKLEY—INNKEEPER
PHONE: 360.378.2783
TOLL FREE: 800.965.0123
EMAIL: RESERVATIONS@TUCKERHOUSE.COM
WEB SITE: WWW.TUCKERHOUSE.COM
ROOMS: 10
RATES: $170–$325
REMARKS: "STAYING AT THE TUCKER HOUSE IS EASY AND FUN! WE LEAVE THE CAR IN ANACORTES AND CAN EASILY WALK TO THE INN AND TO THE GREAT RESTAURANTS IN TOWN. THE STAFF OPENLY SHARES GREAT IDEAS OF WHAT WE CAN DO WHILE ON THEIR BELOVED ISLAND."

Built in 1898 in the Victorian-style the Tucker House Inn was owned b Mr. and Mrs. Clarence M. Tucker. Located one and one half blocks above the ferry landing in a quiet residential neighborhood, this hom is rich in island history.

Mr. Tucker came to San Juan Islan to build and operate a grist mill. Although the mill struggled to stay operation, Clarence became involve in the town's economic growth, serving as County Treasurer. Today the Tucker House Inn welcomes guests at the original Tucker home as well as the Joy House (a second Victorian house built at the turn of the century) and two guest cottage

Innkeepers with a Worldly Vision

A sister property of the neighboring Harrison House Suites, the Tucker House Inn is owned by David Pass and Anna Maria de Freitas. The two visited Friday Harbor in August of 2004 during their 5-year quest to find the perfect B&B opportunity. The next year, the owner of the Tucker House asked David if they were interested in buying this B&B as well.

After some brainstorming, David and Anna Maria realized that the Tucker House was complementary to the Harrison House and they moved forward with the purchase. Having spent years traveling the world to many B&Bs, David and Anna Maria have a deep understanding of the service, surroundings, and the importance of all the little details that go into creating an exceptional guest experience. Along with innkeeper Michael Buckley, their love of entertaining and sharing fine cooked meals is evident throughout your stay.

With manicured gardens, outdoor patios and a large, private deck, the casual elegance of the Tucker House Inn is carried into the many common areas including the sitting room, the solarium and the sun room. All the guest rooms are furnished with antiques and have private baths.

Upper House, Lower House, or a Cottage?

The upper Tucker House (the Joy House) has five guest rooms and four of those rooms have fireplaces as well as two-person Jacuzzi tubs. Hardwood flooring and beautiful oriental rugs complement the decor throughout. The lower Tucker House has three guest suites. Two offer Jacuzzi tubs and one, a two bedroom, two-bath suite has a wood burning stove. The two cottages have private baths, kitchenettes, and wood burning stoves.

Our favorite is the Four Winds suite. This three-room suite offers sweeping views of the town and surrounding hills. From the king bed in the bedroom with French doors leading to a sitting area, to the fireplace and private balcony, to the vaulted ceilings and oversized hand-tiled private bath with a two-person Jacuzzi tub, this suite has everything you need for a romantic stay.

A Page from Anna Maria's Cookbook

Anna Maria's cookbook, La Cucina Anna Maria: Good Life Recipes from San Juan Island, is the result of her culinary experiences and inspires her menu.

Served at the Garden Café in the neighboring Harrison House, the complimentary breakfast consists of four courses—fresh fruit, granola with stirred yogurt, the hot entrée of the day and dessert. Should you fall in love with the granola (as we did!) know that you can purchase it to enjoy back at your house on the mainland.

Friday Harbor House

Location: Friday Harbor 98250 —on San Juan Island
Address: 130 West Street
Host: Berit Keeble
Phone: 360.378.8455
Toll Free: 866.722.7356
Email: fhhouse@rockisland.com
Web Site: www.fridayharborhouse.com
Rooms: 23
Rates: $125–$360
Remarks: "Our room had an incredible view over the yacht harbor and beyond to the islands."

Resting atop a spectacular bluff, Friday Harbor House has a panoramic view of the island's marina, ferry landing, San Juan Channel and Mount Constitution on neighboring Orcas Island. Out of the hustle and bustle of town, while located mere blocks away from all the shopping, dining, galleries and entertainment venues, Friday Harbor is one of the most well-loved destinations in all of the San Juan Islands.

Rooms with a Seagull's View

There are 23 guestrooms in all, including a one-bedroom suite and three town-view suites. Each room features elegant natural wood furnishings and floor-to-ceiling windows that capture dramatic island views. All have a private bath, fireplace with sitting area, and oversized Jacuzzi tub. The European queen bed with custom comforter adds a special touch. (The town-view suites have king beds.)

For the ultimate romantic getaway, ask to have a room with a private balcony. There is something magical about relaxing outside with a glass of wine, watching the last ferry sail into view with its lights reflected on the water. The seagulls' cries from the day have fallen silent and all you hear is water lapping against the docks and occasional laughter drifting from a boat on anchor. In-room amenities include bathrobes, coffee maker, television and refrigerator.

Winemaker Dinners are the Specialty of the House

Friday Harbor House offers a sophisticated culinary experience under the direction of executive chef Matt Colony. With a culinary arts degree from Le Cordon Bleu Culinary Institute in London, he excels in planning and preparing memorable winemaker dinners.

The four- and six-course meals are paired with wines such as Penfolds, Pepper Bridge and Owen-Sullivan wineries. Seasonal farm-fresh island fare and locally caught fish prepared with a global influence make the dinners unforgettable. The Wescott Bay oysters come highly recommended, as are the mussels from Lopez Island (two ferry stops to the east), but Mardi's favorite is the Lopez lamb. Made with fresh local herbs, it knows no rival.

Come morning, the complimentary continental breakfast is extraordinary. From freshly baked scones to the house-made granola, which some believe to be the best on the West coast. Plus, the fruit is always fresh

Island Adventures Abound

The inn's San Juan gathering room is a comfortable lounge area for reading a book by the fire or watching a movie on the 52" plasma screen. Outdoor pursuits include fishing, sailing, sea kayaking, plus whale watching and sea life cruises. For landlubbers, there is great hiking and bicycling on the island (and you might try your hand at geo-teaming).

Island-hopping is an activity you too can enjoy as a walk-on to the frequent ferries that arrive and depart just blocks from Friday Harbor House. At night, Mardi and I enjoy a starlit stroll along the docks. Boaters are buttoning down for the night, or sitting topside for an evening chat with another skipper about their comings and goings around the islands.

LAKEDALE RESORT AT THREE LAKES

LOCATION: FRIDAY HARBOR 98250
—ON SAN JUAN ISLAND
ADDRESS: 4313 ROCHE HARBOR ROAD
HOST: MICHAEL CAWDREY—GENERAL MANAGER
PHONE: 360.378.2350
TOLL FREE: 800.617.2267
EMAIL: INFO@LAKEDALE.COM
WEB SITE: WWW.LAKEDALE.COM
ROOMS: 10 LODGE ROOMS, 6 2-BEDROOM CABINS, 1 3-BEDROOM LAKEHOUSE
RATES: $125–$489
REMARKS: "STAYING AT LAKEDALE CAN CONFUSE YOUR SENSES- IT HAS THE LOOK AND FEEL OF A HIGH MOUNTAIN LAKE-FRONT LODGE AND YET IT IS NESTLED ON A BEAUTIFUL ISLAND ONLY REACHABLE BY FERRY OR FLOAT PLANE."

Whether you're looking for a lake retreat or an island vacation, Lakedale Resort at Three Lakes is an accessible San Juan Island getaway. Its three spring water lakes on 82 acres provide a welcome outdoor escape with many activities available right on the resort grounds, plus a wealth of things to do elsewhere on San Juan Island.

The lakefront accommodations are likely to suit anyone's getaway needs. For those in search of romance, the lodge offers cozy single or double guestrooms.

On the larger side, the cabins can sleep up to six guests, ideal for group vacations or families. For people looking to get especially in touch with the outdoors, 73 tent sites await in the Lakedale Campground. Guests enjoy lake or territorial views from all accommodations.

From Romance to Rustic Rigor

Couples looking for a quiet, romantic retreat may want to know that the ten-room lodge was named by the Fine Living Channel as one of the Top Ten Romantic Getaways in the country. The lodge borders Neva Lake, offering sweeping views, and is decorated lodge style in pine and fir with forest green accents. Guests are warmly greeted by the staff and, on cool days, a roaring fire in the slate fireplace.

Guests may choose from three styles of lodge guestrooms, but for a special occasion, the one to request is room number seven. This two-room suite has a relaxing forest view and plenty of room to relax. Other rooms offer two full-size or one queen bed and overlook the lake. Lodge rooms have a deck, gas fireplace and jetted tub, all designed to help guests absorb the beauty of the lakes and surrounding woodlands. Lodge guests also receive a delicious continental breakfast in the dining room.

The two log cabins near the lake as well as a large three-bedroom, three-bathroom lake house put activities like swimming, fishing and canoeing practically at your doorstep. The cabins have gas fireplaces and are decked out with everything you need, including a full kitchen with cookware and service for six, plus a microwave, coffee maker and toaster. To help guests enjoy a summer night, there is an outdoor fire ring with a grill and picnic table.

Outdoor enthusiasts will appreciate Lakedale's many campsites. They're the perfect place to call home for a few days and reconnect with nature. Also available are "canvas cabins" that provide the experience of camping without having to pitch a tent.

Packing in the Action

There's no shortage of things to do both in the resort and on the island. To help guests take advantage of its many lakes, the Lakedale Resort rents rowboats, canoes and paddleboats. The lakes are well stocked for a quiet day of fishing, and there are walking trails to enjoy the grounds.

Activities abound outside of the resort as well. Mardi always makes a point of shopping in Friday Harbor, which is known for its art galleries, antique shops, bookstores and boutiques. A number of good restaurants and pubs are in town, and for extra adventure, you can book a whale watching tour, rent a bicycle, or take winery or local artisan tours.

Turtleback Farm Inn

Location: Orcas Island 98245
Address: 1981 Crow Valley Road
Hosts: Bill & Susan Fletcher
Phone: 360.376.4914
Toll Free: 800.376.4914
Email: info@turtlebackinn.com
Web Site: www.turtlebackinn.com
Rooms: 11
Rates: $100–$245
Remarks: "We have been dropping in to Turtleback for over 23-years. They were wonderful when we first visited and they just keep getting better with each visit. If there was an advanced course for innkeepers on providing for their guests, I would nominate Bill and Susan as the professors."

So-named for the turtle-shaped land mass rising above West Sound that overlooks this restored 1800's farmhouse, the Turtleback Farm Inn sits on 80 private acres of pastoral fields where sheep graze, ducks dot the ponds and elm-shaded gardens add to the tranquility of this romantic hideaway.

Lovingly restored and meticulously maintained, this two-story green clapboard farmhouse with ivory trim, run by innkeepers Susan and Bill Fletcher, offers intimate accommodations, award winning breakfasts and gracious hosts who truly love being attentive to their guests.

Homegrown Wool Comforters

Inside the farmhouse, the living room boasts a Rumford fireplace, comfortable seating, and a corner game table. Spotless fir floors throughout the inn are softened by Persian rugs. The sunny dining room has a convenient wet bar which is always stocked with special teas, coffees and cocoa.

Each of Turtleback's seven guestrooms has a private bath and is furnished with fine antiques and Early American furniture. All rooms are unique, from the Meadow Room with its expansive view, to the Nook, which is reminiscent of a ship's cabin. Floral print cottons cover the wooly comforters—and the wool is from the backs of the sheep you see grazing outside.

During our visits, we enjoy the nearby cedar Orchard House, which was designed to resemble a barn. The two-story building offers four spacious king-bedded rooms complete with gas fireplaces, sitting/dining areas, full bath with claw-footed soaking tubs, separate large showers, and private decks.

Music with Your Breakfast

Dining room tables are set with fresh white linens, fine china and silver, and a turtle-shaped trivet with a pot of freshly ground coffee or brewed tea. During the summer, there are fresh berries from the island, and the fall brings apples from the trees right on the farm.

While Susan's famed granola offers a fresh start to your morning, the next course of ricotta pancakes with fresh berry sauce puts you in an "island state of mind," especially when enjoyed on the cedar deck overlooking Crow Valley as Celtic harp music drifts out to you from the kitchen. Other equally delicious choices are eggs Benedict, or smoked salmon buckwheat crepe gateau.

Views to Canada

Before setting out for the day, be sure pick up the Fletchers' personal map and ask their advice on what to see and do on Orcas Island. Bicycling, sailing, canoeing, kayaking and golfing on the public course are popular activities. As is strolling through the many shops and galleries in Eastsound Village. If you're looking for Orca whales, try walking along the beach at Obstruction Pass.

Across the road from Turtleback Farm Inn, the new Turtleback Mountain Preserve includes 1,576 acres crisscrossed with hiking trails. Its high meadows and rocky ledges offer breathtaking views of the San Juan and Canadian Gulf Islands.

But the best views are had from atop 2,409 foot Mt. Constitution in nearby Moran State Park. While you can hike it, Mardi and I prefer to take the scenic drive up to this peak, which is the highest point in the San Juan archipelago. The 360 degree views of the surrounding waterways and islands from the stone tower on top of the mountain offer perhaps the most romantic backdrop in all the San Juan Islands. Be sure to bring along your camera!

Inn at Ship Bay

Location: Eastsound 98245 —on Orcas Island
Address: 326 Olga Road
Hosts: Geddes & Mary Anna Martin
Phone: 360.376.5886
Toll Free: 877.276.7296
Email: shipbay@rockisland.com
Web Site: www.innatshipbay.com
Rooms: 11- 10 staterooms and 1 suite
Rates: $125–$295
Remarks: "As we relaxed on our water-view deck, we watched the Head Chef/Inn Owner recycling Salmon carcasses by feeding them to the Bald Eagles, who came swooping down to the bluff; that's recycling Orcas Island style."

With an unobstructed view of the East Sound of Orcas Island, the Inn Ship Bay has been an historic landm on the bluff since 1869. The farmhou the second timber-framed home bu on the island, was originally the hc of Michael Adams, whose apple, pe and plum orchards were part of the cornerstone of this island's historic agricultural economy.

Today, the original farmhouse serves the inn's restaurant while the ten stat rooms and one suite are in surroundi buildings that were built in 2000 to match the vintage farmhouse. Located just one mile from the vill of Eastsound, it offers some of the m comfortable accommodations on Orc

Island (the "horseshoe-shaped island"), which is the largest and most mountainous of all the San Juans.

An unpretentious inn with a casual and relaxed atmosphere, it is still surrounded by acres of fruit bearing trees. It is owned and operated by Geddes and Mary Anna Martin, who have over 20 years of experience in the hospitality field. Looking for a business to run together while raising their own family, they decided to take the inn over when the previous owners retired. A natural segue for them, welcoming guests just comes natural.

Your Home Away from Home

Elegantly furnished in a relaxed, comfortable Northwest style, all rooms have commanding sound views and include propane Franklin stoves, balconies and private bathrooms. Every convenience is offered, including wireless Internet, cable television, and mini-fridges. The suite has a separate living room in addition to the bedroom, an oversized deck, plus a double bathroom with a two person soaking tub.

The king-sized beds (in all rooms) with oversized down pillows and comforter offer a wonderful night's sleep. You'll find the state rooms appointed with a sitting area that has an "overstuffed" love seat and easy chair. It is an especially relaxing chair after a day of shopping in Eastsound village or hiking in nearby Moran State Park. Watching the sun settle over Turtleback Mountain (on the west side of the island) from the privacy of your own room offers a romantic ending to any day.

A complimentary breakfast served each morning features their house made granola, muffins, juices, fresh coffee, plus seasonal fruit, some of which is picked from trees right on the grounds.

Fresh Wholesome Food Prepared Daily

While outdoor waterfront dining with stunning water views is an option in warmer months, year round the Inn at Ship Bay's Dining Room offers seasonal menus that feature fresh, locally farmed products including the herbs and vegetables picked from the gardens onsite.

With prior experience as the Executive Chef at nearby Rosario Resort and in Portland, Oregon, co-owner Geddes Martin has been creating some of the island's most favorite dishes for nearly a decade. Fresh seafood choices are available nightly as are entrees such as grass-fed beef filet, pan seared Draper Valley chicken breast, and roasted breast of duck. Their reasonably-priced wines come from Oregon, Washington and California. All of the breads and desserts are created in-house and most of the produce is supplied from local Island farms.

Mardi especially loves (as do I!) their sourdough bread, which is baked from a starter that is over 100 years old and has been passed generation to generation in Mary Anna's family. A family secret to be shared, it is yours to enjoy whenever you visit your "extended" family at the Inn at Ship Bay.

LOCATION: OLGA 98279, —ON ORCAS ISLAND
ADDRESS: 65 WILLIS LANE
HOSTS: JIM & BETSY NELSON
PHONE: 360.376.4330
EMAIL: BAYSIDE@ORCAS1.COM
WEB SITE: WWW.ORCAS1.COM
ROOMS: 10 (FOUR WATERFRONT COTTAGES PLUS TWO LARGE SUITES AND THREE UPLAND COTTAGES WITH GREAT VIEWS AND BEACH ACCESS IN ADDITION TO ONE EASTSOUND VILLAGE COTTAGE)
RATES: $155–$380
REMARKS: "A PERFECT FAMILY ENVIRONMENT TUCKED INTO A STURDY WELL-EQUIPPED CABIN WITH ACCESS TO A PRIVATE BEACH- THIS IS AS GOOD AS IT GETS!"

Overlooking Rosario Strait, Baysid Cottages sits on a quiet 12-acre waterfront setting offering stunni easterly views toward the islands o Lummi, Cypress and Sinclair with Mt. Baker in the background. Each of the ten cottages has easy access a private beach. In addition, Wister Cottage is separately located in the heart of Eastsound Village on an a of land with a small orchard.

Build over a period of 25 years by t owners Jim and Betsy Nelson (wh bought the property in 1979), thes 11 cottages are the perfect place fo a romantic getaway, a relaxing fam vacation or a side trip for the business traveler.

Cottages for Just Two or the Whole Family

Ranging from 300 to 2000 square feet, the largest is hardly a cottage at all. Aptly named the Beach House, this farmhouse style home with two bedrooms and two baths is situated right on the water. The wood beamed ceilings and hardwood floors give it a warm comfortable feel while the 30-foot-long wall of glass in the sunroom highlights the dramatic view of Mt. Baker and the nearby islands.

Other waterfront cottages include Bayside Cottage and Peapod Cottages (with two adjoining living areas). Upland cottages include Plum Tree, Lummi, and Cypress Cottages and each offer panoramic water views. Unique among this seaside village is The Barn Loft. Located on the upper floor of a converted barn, it greets you with vaulted, beamed ceilings, hardwood floors and many windows looking out to the woods.

Trails Lead to the Beach

Bayside Cottages was carefully designed with the utmost privacy. Every cottage is at least 200 feet away from the next, yet all offer easy access to the private beach through a network of trails on the property. This same attention to design awaits you inside as well, with beautiful and unique furnishings in an antique and traditional style. All cottages have a wood or gas stove (as well as electric heat) and include a kitchen for carefree eating any time of day.

Outside, each offers a private yard or deck with cedar deck chairs and a gas grill that's ready to barbecue a great tasting salmon, hearty steaks or good old fashioned brats served with a favorite Northwest brew. And if you don't feel like cooking, it's a short drive to Café Olga and Artworks, with the many eateries in Eastsound Village just 20 minutes away.

The Rule of Three

Mardi and I have decided that our stay at Bayside Cottages needs to be three nights to take everything in.

Day one is spent shopping and experiencing the arts scene in Eastsound Village. Day two we choose between hiking at the 5,000-acre Moran State Park, Obstruction Pass State Park (if you go, be sure to visit the remote beach accessible only by a hiking trail) or Turtleback Mountain Preserve. Day three we relax at the private beach at the cottages and take in a performance at the Community Theatre at Orcas Center on our last night.

Whatever your routine, be sure to leave your schedule open to enjoy what the locals call "island time." It's what comes natural at Bayside Cottages.

LOCATION: BELLINGHAM 98225
ADDRESS: 804 10TH STREET
HOSTS: J. MICHAEL KEENAN—OWNER & JULIA STINER—OPERATIONS MANAGER
PHONE: 360.756.1005
TOLL FREE: 888.808.0005
EMAIL: INFO@THECHRYSALISINN.COM
WEB SITE: WWW.THECHRYSALISINN.COM
ROOMS: 43
RATES: $179–$299
REMARKS: "THE CHRYSALIS ECLIPSES ANY OTHER LODGING CHOICE IN THE GREATER BELLINGHAM AREA. THE SOARING ARCHITECTURE IS MATCHED UP WITH WARM HOSPITALITY, INCREDIBLE VIEWS OF THE BAY AND REFRESHING SPA AND DINING CHOICES."

Known as Bellingham's hidden treas this luxurious award-winning 43-r inn is steps away from the new Tay Avenue Dock and boardwalk. A pri location, the boardwalk extends ou into Bellingham Bay, connecting gue to Boulevard Park and the historic Fairhaven Shopping District.

Owner/manager Mike Keenan fell in love with the area and opened T Chrysalis as an independent Inn s could retain the creative control of experience offered to guests.

To help set the stage for that experien a striking painting in the main foy measuring seven feet wide by 11-f high, meets your eye as you arrive. Called "Wing", it was commissione by Mike to local artist Astrid Liljegren to illustrate the stage prior to the transformation into a butterfly, for which the Inn is named.

Northwest with an Asian Influence

The Inn's architecture is very open and Northwest with an Asian influence. The living room features a wood burning fireplace and expansive bay views. It opens onto an attached deck that seems to put you within reach of the San Juan Islands towards the west. As you can imagine, the sunsets are spectacular.

Whether you reserve a single room, double room or suite, all offer luxurious appointments beginning with a stunning bay view window seat overlooking sailboat regattas, fishing vessels, soaring eagles and the San Juan Islands rising out of the shimmering waters. Furnished with a contemporary Northwest design, all rooms offer fireplaces, mini bars and two-person soaking tubs (suites have two-person jetted tubs). The slate walk-in showers are a definitive Northwest touch.

On the softer side, you'll find his 'n her robes, cozy slippers, plus luxurious linens and down comforters. No detail is overlooked, right down to the aromatherapy soaps, lotions, and shampoos in your private bath.

A Spa for Your Body and Soul

Rumored to be one of the top 20 luxury coastal spas on the West Coast, Mardi says the Inn's spa services offer a deep relaxation that restores her soul. From massage and facials, to body treatments and hydrotherapy, plus a Vichy shower, steam rooms and a relaxation area, you will simply emerge anew. (Stop by the Hotel Gift Shop and Spa Retail Boutique to bring some of this luxury home with you.)

Three Venues for Eating

With romantic music, idyllic harbor views and a collection of fine art, the dining at the Fino Restaurant is elegant without being pretentious. Executive Chef Scott Jurges has 15 years of experience in prestigious Seattle-area restaurants. He prepares classic European meals, changing his menu with the season, to feature fresh seafood and meats seasoned with herbs, accompanied by local produce.

In addition, the Fino Wine Bar Library offers an intimate fireside lounge for a late-night cheese plate or dessert (my favorite is the rhubarb crème brulee with strawberries). Mardi and I have also enjoyed many an afternoon indulging in appetizers on the deck with an aperitif. That's the beauty of The Chrysalis, it's ready to serve you with the right level of attention that fits your mood—including room service when you'd rather relax in robes instead of donning dinner attire. Come morning, a complimentary hot and cold breakfast buffet is waiting for you in the main dining room.

LOCATION: LUMMI ISLAND 98262
ADDRESS: 2579 WEST SHORE DRIVE NE
HOSTS: RILEY STARKS & JUDY OLSEN
PHONE: 360.758.2620
TOLL FREE: 888.294.2620
EMAIL: RESERVATIONS@WILLOWS-INN.COM
WEB SITE: WWW.WILLOWS-INN.COM
ROOMS: 8
RATES: $120–$350
REMARKS: "THE WILLOWS IS ONE OF THE FEW TRUE COUNTRY INNS IN THE STATE AND ONE OF OUR FAVORITE MID-WINTER PLACES TO STAY, TO WALK THE BEACHES AND TO ENJOY WONDERFUL ORGANIC, FARM-TO-TABLE DINING AND WARM HOSPITALITY."

For years, Mardi and I passed the "Lummi Island" exit on our way to Canada and wondered what the isl was all about. One day our curiosit got the better of us and we took a detour to check it out. That's the da we fell in love with the Willows Inn

Situated eight miles west of Bellingham, Lummi Island is reach by a 10-minute ferry ride. Once ashore, the inn is just three and a half miles from the ferry landing. A 1910 Craftsman bungalow, it is on the west side overlooking Rosar Strait and the San Juan Islands. Sunsets are spectacular.

It All Started with the Farm

The inn is owned and operated by husband-and-wife team Riley Starks and Judy Olsen, who are dedicated to providing tasteful accommodations and genuine hospitality. Together with Chef Craig Miller they are garnering rave reviews from guests and food critics alike.

Riley and Judy moved to Lummi Island in 1992 and founded Nettles Farm, where they began growing organic produce and raising pastured chickens. In 2001 they bought the Willows Inn and realized a long-time dream of offering a farm-to-table restaurant gourmet experience using regional foods to ensure a fresh, wholesome fare. Their breakfast includes mouth watering meals from Nettles Farm fresh eggs and produce- all included in the price of the room.

A lifelong commercial fisherman, Riley's own reefnet-caught salmon are featured in the weekly changing menu. Local live spot prawns are the basis for a Willows summer favorite of "weekend prawns on the deck." In addition to eating on the deck, guests also enjoy meals in the main dining room and at the inn's Taproot Espresso Bar & Pub.

Wonderfully Private Rooms

The Main House offers five guest rooms (full bath and/or showers) that are warmly decorated and private. The Cottage has a kitchenette, gas fireplace, a claw-foot tub and a private deck. There is also a larger Guest House (sleeps 4-6 people) that features a walk-in tiled steam shower and a gas fireplace.

The living room of the main house has a large fireplace surrounded by plenty of seating and large windows overlooking the ever-changing Rosario Strait and the San Juan Islands. Throughout the inn you'll find displays by local artists, sculptures in the gardens and frescos on the patio walls.

The Art of Living

A bike ride on the seven-mile island loop is a great way to work up your appetite for dinner. Hiking trails weave through the woods and a leisurely stroll along the inn's private beach is definitely in order.

From August to September, Orca whales can be seen right from the inn's deck and bald eagles often soar overhead. Kayaking comes natural here. In addition, the inn offers excursions in their own six person runabout to neighboring islands for picnics and exploring.

Once you get back on land, you can enjoy a massage or simply relax in the outdoor hot tub. For Mardi and me, the main attraction having a well-mixed cocktail on the deck while anticipating dinner. Plan on leisurely spending two-hours over a remarkable dinner as the world visibly rotates around you.

Abendblume Pension

Location: Leavenworth 98826
Address: 12570 Ranger Road
Hosts: Renee & Randy Sexauer
Phone: 509.548.4059
Toll Free: 800.669.7634
Email: info@abendblume.com
Web Site: www.abendblume.com
Rooms: 7
Rates: $139–$239
Remarks: "This is by far the most authentic lodging experience in this Austrian-flavored community."

The town of Leavenworth in the Cascade Mountains is home to a tr Bavarian Village that, season after season, continues to draw Mardi a me back. Each excursion fills our fi (and hearts) with stories to tell anc a recent find to share. Abendblume Pension is one of the rarest finds o

Located in an open area to appreci the serenity of the mountains, but still close to all the town has to off this award-winning old world Bava inn is authentic in architecture anc service alike.

Designed, and largely built by proprietors Randy and Renee Sexa (whose travels throughout Austria inspired the inn's design),

Abendblume sits on the very land where Renee was raised. Its handmade lobby doors and immense wood pillars set the stage for the spectacular architecture inside.

Beyond the doors, you'll find old world archways, carved wood walls and ceilings, plus hand forged iron stair railings on the elegant curved stairway. A loving tribute to the Austrian chalet, Abendblume (meaning Evening Flowering) is as romantic as it is luxurious.

Every Room Tells its Own Story

The inn's seven rooms are namesakes for nature (from Rosengarten to Tannenbaum) and fairy tales (including Snow White). No two are alike, but all are spacious with an accent on comfort and privacy.

Each room (or suite) is a retreat into a distant time and place. Warm wood windows with window seats offer a prime spot to relax with a good book or to pen a postcard. All rooms have private baths and showers (some with heated tile floors) and most offer a Whirlpool tub and a fireplace (electric, gas or wood burning).

Whether you choose a room with French Doors opening to a terrace, or one with a private balcony overlooking the pond and mountains, you'll be pampered in luxury with fine ironed linens, European down comforters, and duvets.

Breakfast is the Main Event

There is no better way to begin your day than with fruhstuck served in the traditional Austrian breakfast room. This full spread of fresh fruits, meats, and cheeses is prepared every morning along with a delicious homemade granola and muesli.

But the highlight is their famous Aebleskivers (Danish pancakes) topped with homemade apple syrup. French press coffee and teas are served right at your table.

A Four Season Destination

In summer, Mardi and I enjoy the town's stage production under the stars in the amphitheater. Fall offers Octoberfest, and winter ushers in the Tree Lighting Festival. Shopping goes year-round. For the more active set, there's golfing, river rafting, skiing, dog sledding and more.

For every season, a romantic ending for your day back at Abendblume is a soothing in-room massage and the Chateaubriand dinner for two served in the privacy of your candlelit room.

Before You Go

For a truly romantic way to begin your stay, call in advance to have a cheese basket or luxurious monogrammed robes (100% Egyptian cotton, of course) waiting in your room when you arrive (additional charge applies). It's the best way to understand the meaning of Abendblume's mantra of wir verwahnen sie... meaning "we spoil you".

Run of the River Inn and Refuge

Location: Leavenworth 98826
Address: 9308 E Leavenworth Road
Hosts: Monty & Karen Turner
Phone: 509.548.7171
Toll Free: 800.288.6491
Email: info@runoftheriver.com
Web Site: www.runoftheriver.com
Rooms: Six Suites plus Ravenwood Lodge
Rates: $220–$425
Remarks: "Guys- the next time your wife wants a weekend away — quick- make the reservation at Run of the River- you'll be in heaven. You can sit on the bank of the river, or hike right from the front door. The inn has large comfortable rooms and there is not a dainty little Victorian chair in sight- oh and by the way your wife will love it too."

A luxurious Northwest lodge, deer among the top 100 Wilderness Lodges by Outside Magazine Run of the River Inn & Refuge offers guests the allure of its natural alpi surroundings coupled with all the comforts guests seek today. Perche on a seasonal high-water channel c the Icicle River and surrounded on two sides by a wildlife refuge, the well-situated inn begs to be shared and appreciated.

Owners Karen and Monty are forn teachers with a love of the Northw and the Icicle Valley. They enjoy hiking, biking, cross-country skiin and an occasional round of golf, an they take particular joy in helping guests find the best places to find any activity they would like as part of their experience at the inn.

In fact, the inn's best amenity may well be its active innkeepers providing accurate recreation and tourism information. They'll also provide outdoor equipment to help you get the most from your stay: mountain and tandem bikes, snowshoes, day packs, hiking sticks, and complimentary trail passes.

Wing It in the Cascades

Run of the River's breakfast area is an ideal spot to view wildlife from the large picture windows looking over the refuge, which is managed by the state of Washington. Though only a mile from the Bavarian-styled town of Leavenworth, guests feel far removed and wrapped in nature.

A touch of whimsy adorns the Run of the River in the collection of classic bicycles, wooden skis, snowshoes and sleds.

Six suites, beautifully decorated in classic Northwest lodge style welcome guests in the main lodge. Each "adventure suite" is spacious and private, with fireplaces, double whirlpool bubs surrounded in river rock and hand-hewn log beds. The private decks allow for bird-watching from the comfort of your own room and each deck features a double swing and a "Jay Tray" on which to place the peanuts provided to attract wildlife. Conveniently, the owners provide binoculars and birding guides in the rooms.

Separate and adjacent is the new Ravenwood Lodge, built in 1992 and completely remodeled in 2006. It is an ideal getaway nest for two with its picture-perfect views of the Enchantments, river rock fireplace, full kitchen, and an overwhelming feeling of Northwest bounty.

The views are right out to nature: squirrels, chipmunks, and many different kinds of birds. The unblemished view is of the Enchantments, which beckon guests to a hike or at least a relaxing few minutes lingering on the log swing in the sunshine or the cedar hot tub on the deck in the night time.

From Washington's Fruit Basket

Breakfast begins with a freshly whipped organic yogurt, and then follows with platters of fresh fruit. The breakfast entrees are healthy and fresh—in fact, the cookbook is the inn's number one take-home piece. The menu takes advantage of the seasonally available fruit.

Run of the River delivers a special combination of privacy and nature. Because it's a smaller inn, guests quickly get on a first-name basis—and they return year after year to reconnect with the Valley, themselves and each other.

LOCATION: LEAVENWORTH 98826
—IN THE MOUNTAINS ABOVE THE VILLAGE
ADDRESS: PO BOX 687
HOSTS: BRAD & KATHY SCHMIDT
PHONE: 509.548.7077
TOLL FREE: 800.414.2378
EMAIL: INFO@MTHOME.COM
WEB SITE: WWW.MTHOME.COM
ROOMS: 10 IN MAIN LODGE & 2 CABINS
RATES:
SUMMER: $130–$360
WINTER: $300–$530
REMARKS: "NESTLED IN THE MOUNTAINS ABOVE LEAVENWORTH AND OVERLOOKING A BROAD MEADOW. THIS FOUR-SEASON RESORT HAS IT ALL- FULL DAYS OF ACTIVITIES, GOURMET MEALS AND LUXURIOUS ROOMS TO RE-CHARGE YOUR BATTERIES FOR THE NEXT DAY."

Nestled in a 20-acre alpine valley
at an elevation of 1,000 feet abov
the valley floor, the Mountain Ho
Lodge offers the ultimate romant
rendezvous. While only two mile
from the Bavarian-themed villag
of Leavenworth, its location is so
secluded that guests are brought
by the lodge's own Snowcat in wi

In this playground of the gods de
in the Wenatchee National Fores
outdoor activities span every sea
the cuisine is superb and your to
relaxation is assured. Whether yo
reserve one of 10 guest rooms in t
lodge, or choose a private cabin, you
will experience a unique blend of h
class luxury and high country

adventure in a resort destination setting.

A Northwest Lodge That's a Dream Come True

Your hosts are Brad and Kathy Schmidt, two professionals from different coasts who exchanged their advertising/banking corporate lifestyles for the opportunity to pursue a dream they so often talked about.

Built in 1984, the lodge's open spaces seem to connect you directly to the outdoors. The glass walls of the vaulted dining room overlook the Stuart Mountain Range. The entertainment room offers surround sound movies, plush leather chairs for lounging and tables with games to play, but my favorite is the reading loft with comfy chairs and a spotting scope to enjoy the inspiring view through the windows.

All rooms offer a private bath. Some also have private balconies, fireplaces and Jacuzzi spas. Each room is themed to the outdoors (the Cascade Suite, the Mountain Trout, etc.) and is outfitted with contemporary Northwest furnishings. Wireless Internet is available throughout the resort.

The two custom built cabins are atop their own ridge. Intended for just two people, each cabin features the ultimate in privacy, spectacular views of the Cascades, a hand carved king size bed, private deck, river rock fireplace, refrigerator and indoor river rock spa tub.

Seasonal Menu of the Northwest's Rich Bounty

The complementary full gourmet breakfast comes with fresh fruits, their signature Mountain Home Lodge Granola and a Chef's selection. Maybe it's the rarified air, but Executive Chef Thomas Obregon's Northwest Eggs Benedict with smoked wild salmon and lemon hollandaise is the best I've ever had (and Mardi loves his pumpkin pancakes with warm organic orchard apples and lodge-made cider syrup).

In the winter season (mid-November through March) lunch and a four-course dinner are also included with the cost of your lodging. Drinks are extra (primarily Northwest wines and micro brewed beers/ales). Year-round there are treats such as freshly baked cookies, seasonal fruit and Lodge blended trail mix.

First Class Resort Amenities

Onsite you will find a heated seasonal pool, lighted tennis court, basketball, volleyball and 40 miles of trails for hiking and mountain biking. Three excellent golf courses are nearby and Leavenworth offers wine tasting, shopping, galleries and more.

Once the snow starts to fly, the lodge has equipment for cross country skiing, snowshoeing, guided snowmobiles tours and sledding on their own 1700 foot toboggan run. Year-round, the outdoor Jacuzzi offers welcomed relaxation and a wondrous star show above your head. No matter what your sign is, you'll be sure to thank your lucky stars that you discovered the natural beauty and serenity of this romantic mountain resort.

LOCATION: WINTHROP 98862
ADDRESS: 604 PATTERSON LAKE ROAD
HOST: BRIAN CHARLTON—GENERAL MANAGER
PHONE: 509. 996.2211
TOLL FREE: 800. 572.0493
EMAIL: SUNMTN@SUNMOUNTAINLODGE.COM
WEB SITE: WWW.SUNMOUNTAINLODGE.COM
ROOMS: 96 MOUNTAINTOP GUEST ROOMS, 16 LAKESIDE CABINS
RATES: $160–$390
REMARKS: "RECENTLY WE GATHERED IN FRONT OF THE LARGE WINDOW IN OUR ROOM WATCHING THE SUNSET WHEN WE NOTICED A DEER AND HER FAWN JUST YARDS AWAY STARING UP AT US. THIS INTIMATE CLOSENESS WITH NATURE IS AN EVERYDAY EXPERIENCE AT SUN MOUNTAIN LODGE."

Guests come from far and wide to t Sun Mountain Lodge for its elegant mountaintop setting, with 360-deg views of the North Cascade Mount and Methow Valley. Located on 3,000 acres bordering the Okanoga National Forest, Sun Mountain Loc offers a full complement of activitie right on the resort grounds, includi cross-country skiing, mountain bik and horseback riding.

A GREAT RESORT IN THE MAKING

The spectacular Sun Mountain Lodge began as the dream of a youn man who rode through northern Washington as a youth. Seeking to share the experience of the land wi others, he opened the original Sun Mountain Lodge in 1968. The location was the top of a 3,000-foot high mountain with sweeping views of surrounding mountains, wilderness and valleys. The lodge was specifically designed to blend in with its surroundings using materials such as huge l ocal boulders, fossil-imbedded stones and mammoth timbers.

When the lodge changed hands two decades later, the new owners renovated and expanded it to meet the needs of today's traveler. Following in the footsteps of the original lodge, the "new" resort uses magnificent wooden beams made of Douglas fir and an Idaho quartz stone floor, successfully upholding the original's rustic elegance.

All Rooms with a View

All rooms at the Lodge deliver views of North Cascade Mountains or the Methow Valley. The rooms serve to help guests connect with their beautiful natural surroundings, so they are smoke free and television free. The décor is a comfortable, contemporary look, and much of the wood furniture is locally made. Rooms have king or queen beds, and some also include a twin daybed. Many rooms have wood-burning or gas fireplaces, sitting areas, mini refrigerators and private decks.

Although any visit to Sun Mountain Lodge is a special one, guests with a particular occasion to celebrate may want to reserve one of the Mt. Robinson guest rooms. They set a romantic mood with king beds, jetted tubs, gas fireplaces, mini bars and a private deck where you can enjoy a glass of wine and the seasonally changing view.

Taste the Region

If the scenery and accommodations aren't enough to satisfy, the food most certainly is. The restaurant's Northwest regional ingredients, with a focus on the freshest product at hand, distinguish the Sun Mountain Lodge dining experience, which is worthy of its many awards.

Chef Patrick Miller brings years of experience from celebrated Seattle dining spots including the Four Seasons Olympic Hotel, now the Fairmont Olympic, and the Georgian Room. His menu includes naturally grown herbs and vegetables from the adjacent Sunny M Farm, tenderloin of Washington state beef, and mushrooms foraged from the Cascade Mountains that surround the lodge. The wine list will appease any oenophile, with a 5,000 bottle cellar featuring many award winning Northwest wines, some of which can only be found at the Resort.

Mardi and I find that the Sun Mountain Lodge makes it easy for guests to enjoy the outdoor beauty in every season, from sleigh rides to boating and more, all with the highest experiences of courtesy, charm, character, calm and cuisine. This is our favorite place to bring out-of the-region guests to experience the Washington Mountains. It's nothing short of extraordinary—just like the views.

BIRCHFIELD MANOR COUNTRY INN

LOCATION: YAKIMA 98901
ADDRESS: 2018 BIRCHFIELD ROAD
HOSTS: BRAD MASSET & FAMILY
PHONE: 509.452.1960
TOLL FREE: 800.375.3420
EMAIL: RESERVATIONS@BIRCHFIELDMANOR.COM
WEB SITE: WWW.BIRCHFIELDMANOR.COM
ROOMS: 11
RATES: $119–$219
REMARKS: "THIS RENOWNED COUNTRY INN HAS ADDED NEW ROOMS WHICH MATCH THE EXQUISITE DINING EXPERIENCE."

Picture a 1910 farmhouse two miles from town, surrounded by pasture, fields, and a bird sanctuary, set agai the tranquility of the Yakima Valley Wine Country. That's Birchfield Ma Country Inn. Located in the first American Viticulture Area designat in Washington, this region's excelle wine attracts many visitors every ye

Originally the main house to a 15,0 acre sheep ranch, today it is a B&B and gourmet restaurant owned and maintained by the Masset family along with Tim Newbury. A cottage house built in 1995 stands next to t original farmhouse, offering a total nine single rooms and two suites to welcome guests.

Two Chefs to Please Your Palette

Larger than a typical B&B yet smaller than a hotel, Birchfield Manor has the accommodations of a four star hotel while retaining the warm feeling of a gracious home. It was the perfect property in the perfect setting that the Masset family had always dreamed of owning. With two chefs in the family—Wil Masset received his culinary training in St. Moritz, Switzerland and his son Brad completed the Culinary Arts program at Seattle Community College—Birchfield Manor offers a multi-course dining experience unique to central Washington.

A mix of Country French and Victorian décor, the inn offers a relaxed feeling throughout the common areas and the rooms. Eight of the nine rooms have whirlpool tubs and some offer gas fireplaces plus a private deck or patio. The two penthouse suites have television. All rooms in the house and cottage have private baths and wireless Internet.

Take a Tour of the Valley

Looking out your window, the panoramic views of the valley and the surrounding hills are dramatic and appear to continually change as the sun moves across the sky. Park like grounds surround the outdoor pool.

Beyond the manor's grounds, local wineries dot the countryside. Wil or Brad were happy to personalize a tour of the local wineries for Mardi and me, and direct us to roadside stands for fresh fruit and vegetables. Golf enthusiasts can talk to Tim about tee times at the best golf courses around. Other activities nearby include hiking and rafting.

From the Dining Room to Wine Cellar

If wine tasting, gourmet cuisine and romantic evenings are high on your list of priorities, you'll feel right at home at Birchfield Manor. The complementary award-winning breakfast begins with homemade granola, followed up by a savory chicken and wild mushroom frittata.

Multi-course dinners are served Thursday, Friday and Saturday. Any evening you can enjoy a hors d'oeuvre plate, dinner, dessert or handmade chocolates in your room. My favorite dinner is the fresh filet of King Salmon wrapped in puff pastry and baked. Served with Yakima Valley Chardonnay sauce, it is an innovative and delicious twist to a Northwest favorite. For dessert, chocolate lovers will swoon over the triple Belgian chocolate mousse torte with fresh raspberry sauce.

In addition to the main dining room, dinner is also served in the wine cellar. A romantic setting, it is perfect for an intimate dinner. With an extensive selection of award winning Washington wines (including Wine Press NW Award of Excellence, Wine Spectator Award of Excellent and others), you're sure to discover a new favorite to take home with you.

Marcus Whitman Hotel & Conference Cente

Location: Walla Walla 99362
Address: Six West Rose Street
Hosts: Kyle Mussman—owner & general manager
Phone: 509.525.2200
Toll Free: 866.826.9422
Email: info@marcuswhitmanhotel.com
Web Site: .marcuswhitmanhotel.com
Rooms: 91 guest rooms, 16 of those are luxury suites. An additional 36 rooms will be open in fall of 2007
Rates: $109–$275
Remarks: "The restoration of the Whitman has been a masterful blend of the historic with the most up-to-date services and amenities."

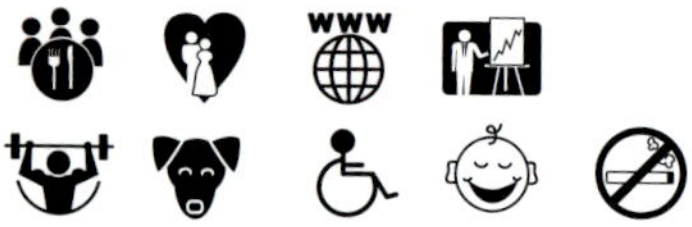

An icon of Walla Walla, the Marcus Whitman Hotel and Conference Center is a timeless and elegant accommodation for a romantic visi to the area's fine wineries. Its perioc décor and special service always ensure a pleasant and memorable s

The Marcus Whitman was named f missionaries Marcus and Narcissa Whitman, who moved to the Walla Walla Valley during the 1830's and welcomed tired travelers making their way along the Oregon Trail. The missionaries were killed in 184 When locals began to talk of openi a luxury hotel during the 1920's, however, the legendary hospitality these missionaries naturally inspired them. The hotel was partly funded by selling subscriptions to individuals and families throughout the area, making the construction of the hotel a true community project.

After its opening in 1928, the hotel quickly became a center of top quality accommodations and fine food. Over the years it received many famous guests, such as President Dwight D. Eisenhower, Vice President Lyndon B. Johnson, Louie Armstrong and Shirley Temple. By the 1990's the hotel had begun to show its age. In 1999 a new owner, Kyle Mussman, undertook a full restoration of the original tower and an adjacent property, bringing them together with the addition of 10,000 square feet of conference meeting space. The hotel reopened in spring 2001.

A Rich Tradition

Designed by Sherwood D. Ford of Seattle, the hotel reflects the 1920's in its architecture and décor. The hotel has several ballrooms, both new and original. The Empire Room in particular shows off the hotel's history with restored original details such as the stained glass skylight, chandeliers and wall sconces. The hotel's art collection includes paintings of the Whitmans, as well as works of art created by the hotel's Executive Chef, Bear Ullman. In the hotel's restaurant guests may notice Chef Bear's hand-crafted wooden bowls and platters in use bearing a salad or wedges of cheese.

The hotel offers 91 guest rooms, including 16 two-room luxury suites located in the historic tower. All rooms are richly decorated in Renaissance-style dark browns and burgundies, with hand-crafted Italian furniture. I am especially partial to the luxury suites. Not only are they located in the historic tower, but the suite's parlor living room is great for relaxing. The sleeping area features a king-sized bed and desk, and the oversized bathroom includes full-sized bathtub, as well as large bath sheets and bathrobes.

Creative Foods of the Pacific Northwest

Each morning guests may partake in a complementary full buffet breakfast served in The Marc Restaurant. The selections are many and include pastries, fruits, potatoes, eggs and breakfast meats.

With its rich and gleaming wood interior, The Marc Restaurant has been voted as the most romantic place to dine in the area, and dinners at the hotel even surpass the excellent breakfast. Chef Bear's artistry extends beyond his impressive wood art. He crafts delicious dinners using house-made breads and fresh local ingredients, including wines and cheeses from the area. Mardi and I enjoy the regular winemaker's dinners, in which foods are paired with wines from the Walla Walla region. Such special meals are well suited to this stylish, historic venue.

Fat Duck Inn

Location: Walla Walla 99362
Address: 527 Catherine Street
Hosts: Alexa Palmer & Chef Charles Maddrey
Phone: 509.526.DUCK (3825)
Toll Free: 888. 526.8718
Email: info@fatduckinn.com
Web Site: www.fatduckinn.com
Rooms: 4
Rates: $100–$185
Remarks: "This cozy and intimate inn has it all- great rooms, dining and wonderfully sociable hosts."

Located on an upscale, tree-lined st
in an historic neighborhood in the h
of Washington's wine country, this
impeccably remodeled 1928 Craftsr
offers an atmosphere of discrete lux
blended with casual informality. Bu
true hallmark hails from the five-cc
gourmet dinners prepared nightly b
chef and co-owner Charles Maddrey

Originally from the Chesapeake Bay
area, Charles' cooking is infused wit
regional influences from his prior
chef experiences in Charleston, New
Orleans and Atlanta. Coming to Sea
in 1999, he worked at Campagne in
Seattle Pike Place Market before bei
recruited to Gene's Ristorante by th
owner Alexa Palmer.

A Fresh Start

In December 2006, the pair decided to simplify their lives. Hearing the buzz of the booming wine industry in Walla Walla, Alexa sold Gene's Ristorante and they headed east to open the Fat Duck Inn. To this couple it's all about the food and wine.

Their first focus, however, was to restore the home to its former original elegance. Cherry hardwood gleams throughout the inn, accented by a mix of French and American antiques (decidedly "anti-Victorian", the mission-style furnishings are "man-friendly"). The four suites, accommodating from two to six guests, all have fireplaces and private baths with luxurious bedding, linens, robes, and slippers. Plus they all afford their guests complete privacy.

Four Suites and a Guest House

While my favorite is the upstairs Merganser suite (with a handsome sleigh bed and commanding territorial view), the main floor Gadwall and Pintail suites plus the downstairs Widgeon suite are equally as private and well-appointed. In addition, just two blocks away, the Fat Duck Guest House is a turn of the century three-bedroom Victorian Bungalow. With hot tub, deck, gas BBQ, large private fenced backyard (and doggy-door for well-behaved four-footed family members) it's an inviting home the whole family can enjoy.

Dinner is Served at Seven O'Clock

All guests are invited to a complimentary continental breakfast (the homemade fig jam and ginger-peach preserves are a must-have!) but the main event is dinner. On summer nights it is served in the most romantic spot of the inn—the outside patio (which seats 20). It is a true five-course affair orchestrated with a fiery sunset.

Our favorite appetizer is a crab, ahi tuna and cured salmon timbale, followed by an asparagus bisque soup. The duck and cheese ravioli is savory. And for a main entrée, the roasted pork tenderloin with braised bacon and truffled potatoes is superb. It's an amazing dinner paired perfectly with the local wine varietals. And the Grand Marnier crème brulee is a dessert that knows no equal.

A Tour of the Valley

For adventure beyond the grounds of this wonderful inn, nearby activities include leisurely bike rides, rounds of golf and strolling through downtown shops. But, by far, the most popular activity is wine touring. As Mardi likes to say, the Fat Duck Inn is located 273 miles east of Seattle only five miles west of Napa Valley.

Arrive by 5:00 p.m. for their complimentary Wine Hour (a different wine from one of 90 local wineries is poured every night) and you may find yourself indulging in the romantic notion of starting your own winery in a not-too-distant valley.

Basel Cellars Estate Winery

Location: Walla Walla, 99362
Address: 2901 Old Milton Highway
Host: Becky Brammer
Phone: 509.522.0200
Toll Free: 888.259. WINE
Email: info@baselcellars.com
Web Site: www.baselcellars.com
Room: One freestanding suite
Rates: $250 plus a $50 non-member fee
Remarks: "This is the ultimate private lodging experience, staying in your own pool-side cabana on top of a hill surrounded by an estate vineyard in the heart of Walla Walla Valley Wine Country."

At the base of the Blue Mountains on 87 acres of landscaped property (including 26 acres of vineyards), Basel Cellars Estate Winery offers a romantic escape far from the ordinary. In full production since th 2002 harvest, the facility produces award-winning wines with a focus on Bordeaux-style blends, Syrah and Cabernet Sauvignon and Merlot.

This sprawling estate began when owner Greg Basel retired from a ma construction company and moved h wife Becky and their family to Walla Walla. There he planted a 32-acre vineyard called Pheasant Run. Greg and Becky will soon be adding an additional Estate Vineyard to the Basel Cellars Estate.

Basel Cellars is a true wine country resort. Their promise to offer guests the "Never Ending Wine Experience" is exceeded in every way. Estate manager Becky Brammer, who has been with them since day one, ensures guests receive the same quality of care that goes into making the wine.

The American Lodge Comes to the Northwest

Basel Cellar's main building is an awe-inspiring design replicating the great American lodge. And if you've even seen Yosemite's Awahnee Lodge, or Mt. Hood's Timberline Lodge you know what I mean. Rustic but elegant, this 13,800 square foot lodge features handcrafted woodwork, natural stone masonry, and an abundance of windows in the style of the Pacific Northwest.

The lodge offers seven luxurious bedrooms with queen beds and a grand master suite with a king bed. In order to rent the entire lodge, you must join the Basel Cellars Wine Club. (See their web site for information on joining.) For the individual couple there is a separate poolside Cabana with one guest room (king bed) and private bath. In addition to the pool, all guests have access to the gourmet kitchen, hot tub, sauna, theme bar, commercial outdoor grills, and more.

A complimentary continental breakfast of fruit, bagels, cream cheese plus juice and coffee is available. There is an informal dining room (a formal dining room is available for private catered dinners or for your personal use). But the most inspired room is the Harley-themed entertainment hall. It's a room dedicated to the Easy Rider in all of us!

Outside, Basel Cellars offers acres of landscaped gardens, patios and vineyards overlooking the Walla Walla River. It's a stunning setting with flowing streams, waterfalls and garden-lined paths for leisurely early morning walks or romantic evening strolls at sunset.

While staying at Basel Estate, the valley offers a beautiful historic downtown shopping district where you can enjoy dinner or a show before coming back to your gated estate come nightfall.

Wine Tasting is a Daily Ritual

The winemaking facility is housed in a 9,600 square foot subterranean structure. The wine tasting room is open seven days a week from 10:00 a.m. to 4:00 p.m. With so many wines to appreciate, Mardi and I have spent many afternoons here. The tasting room gift shop offers the budding sommelier a great selection of books, wine glasses and more to take home. The tasting room also has a large patio with 180 degree view of the Blue Mountains for bringing your own lunch or having one of our local merchant lunches from Basel Cellars.

DAVENPORT HOTEL AND TOWER

LOCATION: SPOKANE, 99201
ADDRESS: 10 SOUTH POST STREET
HOSTS: WALT & KAREN WORTHY-OWNERS
PHONE: 509.455.8888
TOLL FREE: 800.899.1482
EMAIL: INFO@THEDAVENPORTHOTEL.COM
WEB SITE: WWW.THEDAVENPORTHOTEL.COM
ROOMS: 283 IN HOTEL AND 328 IN NEW TOWER
RATES: $219–$2,500
REMARKS: "SAVING THE SHUTTERED DAVENPORT WAS A NOBLE UNDERTAKING, RESULTING IN THE MOST REMARKABLE RESTORATION IN WESTERN AMERICA."

When people in Spokane say "I'll meet you at the fireplace," they mea the one at the Davenport Hotel in t heart of the city. Lit by hotelier Loui Davenport in 1914 when the hotel first opened, the fireplace had been constantly kept burning until the hotel closed in 1985.

In 2002, present-day owners Walt a Karen Worthy reopened the hotel a re-lit the fireplace as a tribute to Lou Davenport's standards of hospitalit A romance story from the start, Wa and Karen dated at the Davenport Hotel in 1970. Never did they drear they would one day buy it, restore it and operate it. It is their only hotel, and it is luxurious. So much so that it was selected by Conde Nast as a "Top 100" and "Gold List" hotel.

Attracts a Well-Healed Clientele

A member of Historic Hotels of America, the Davenport served as home to seven sitting U.S. Presidents and numerous celebrities, including Charles Lindbergh, Amelia Earhart, Cher, Jerry Seinfeld and Neil Diamond. Today it's recognized as a peer to the top hotels in the world—a remarkable achievement considering the short time it's been re-opened.

Florentine in style, the hotel was the largest and finest commission of the architect Kirtland Cutter. While the lobby is reminiscent of an Italian piazza (complete with a central fountain and pillared streetlights), my favorite room is the Hall of the Doges. Inspired by the Palace of the Doges in Venice, it was rescued intact from the original Davenport's restaurant and re-positioned in the new Davenport Hotel.

A View from Every Room

While suites include fireplaces, all rooms are luxurious and offer city views and/or South Hill views, private baths, fine linens, and custom made Davenport Pillow Top mattresses. Many also feature hand-painted original oils. The room décor is European classic in the Hotel and international travel in the newly opened Tower.

Our favorite room is the Presidential Suite, with a balcony affording Southwesterly views of Sunset Hill and the South Hill. Other Suites we can recommend are the Governors Suite, Davenport Suite, Cutter Suite, Parlor Suite and Honeymoon Suite (and it's not just for newly weds!)

The Birthplace of the King Louis Salad

With three different venues for eating, Mardi and I are continually finding new favorite dishes. The Palm Court Grill open for breakfast, lunch and dinner is all about fresh seafood, with an extensive wine list and homemade desserts (my weakness is their hot fudge sundae sprinkled with homemade soft peanut brittle). But a must-have is the signature Crab Louie, named for the original hotel owner. And yes, this king of salads originated in this very hotel!

In the Tower, the Safari Room Fresh Grill offers a full menu for all three meals and also serves a late night menu. For music and after dinner drinks, the Peacock Room is lively and fun.

Voted Spokane's "Best place to have a drink!", one of their excellent martinis is the perfect end to an afternoon of shopping at nearby River Park Square or strolling along Riverfront Park. And if your stay includes a Sunday, Mardi and I highly recommend the Champagne Sunday brunch in the Hotel.

Montvale Hotel

Location: Spokane 99201
Address: 1005 W. 1st Avenue
Hosts: Rob Brewster—Owner & Doug Griepp—General Manager
Phone: 509.747.1919
Toll Free: 1.86.MONTVALE
Email: info@montvalehotel.com
Web Site: www.montvalehotel.com
Rooms: 36
Rates: $119–$295
Remarks: "The impressive atrium is quite a pleasant surprise to first-time guests of this impeccably renovated downtown hotel."

Built in 1899, the Montvale Hotel is Spokane's oldest standing hotel building and is listed on the Nationa Register of Historic Places. The Spok River and Falls are just two blocks to the north. The hotel's three-story façade retains its classic style, while interiors have been recently rejuven along with the neighborhood, creati a hotel of exceptional character and comfortable accommodations.

In the heart of downtown in the arts district, the Montvale is truly a destination hotel located within a block of the revitalized Fox Theater, Big Easy concert hall and Ella's Supp Club jazz venue. Many art galleries a restaurants are accessible within a fe blocks of the hotel.

Accommodation with Panache

The Montvale Building's red brick and large windows are typical of western American buildings of the late 1800's, while the large atrium and grand stairs give the feel of a major city hotel. The Montvale was built in 1899 and completed its conversion into a boutique hotel in 2005.

The overall décor is a mixture of American and European antiques and rugs, accompanied by more modern furniture. Influenced by his year of living in Vienna, Austria, owner Rob Brewster sought to create a place that has European style without feeling overly European. This balance of old Europe and turn-of-the-century western design permeates the Montvale and its restaurant, the Catacombs Pub.

A focus of the interior is its beautiful second and third floor atrium with an enormous 70-foot by 20-foot skylight. The two-story atrium is packed with old wooden bookcases, antique furniture and the owner's unique art collection. Among the art collection is a small painting created by his mother in the late 1960's.

Nocturnal Spectacle

The 36 guestrooms include queens, deluxe kings, parlor suites with Murphy beds, double queens and two outstanding presidential suites. All rooms have private bathrooms, some with jetted tubs. Enhancing the comfort of the rooms are their 11-foot ceilings and over-sized bathrooms with Gilchrist & Soames bath products. From many rooms guests may appreciate striking views of downtown Spokane, especially at night.

When staying at the Montvale, Mardi and I seek out the large corner rooms, which have a separate seating area and fireplace. Another special room is the presidential suite, which has an original painting of Dwight D. Eisenhower painted as he sat for the artist. The room was dedicated by Eisenhower's granddaughter in 2005.

Not Your Average Pub

For dining options, be sure to enjoy the casual-yet-memorable Catacombs Pub, an old European style underground restaurant with large exposed wood beams and iron chandlers. Its wood-fired pizza stone oven uses the original stone and mortar work from the turn of the century and produces an excellent thin-crust chicken cashew pesto pizza.

When dining here, be sure to save room for unusual and decadent desserts. I indulge in the Nutella Hazelnut chocolate calzone, while Mardi likes to order the s'mores and make them just the way she likes them with the table-top roaster. After dinner, guests may achieve the ultimate Montvale experience, sipping wine in front of the fireplace in the candle-lit atrium, looking up through the skylight at the stars.

We hope your travels to the Special Places of Washington will create your own special memories. Here are a few of ours.

- Enjoying the incredible breakfast at the Shelburne Inn while David plans out what we should see that day.
- Walking the beach by the Quinault Resort and reflecting on all the early history that happened on this same beach.
- Sitting in the back yard at Colette's and looking north at the lights of Victoria as they slowly come on at dusk.
- Driving up to Lost Mountain Lodge, not knowing what to expect and being stunned to find such a wonderful place hidden in the Olympics.
- Following BJ and Frank at BJ's Garden Gate as they walk us through their hand-crafted gardens and hoping Mardi would not be inspired to also plant 25,000 bulbs in our garden.
- Having our first cup of coffee while sitting on the James House front lawn and watching the ferries arrive and depart from the docks below us.
- Walking from the Bishop Victorian Hotel through Port Townsend to explore the bunkers above historic Fort Warden.
- Waking up in the Inn at Port Hadlock and watching the sunrise over Port Townsend Bay.
- Driving down the private hill-hugging, tree-shaded drive and coming in under the impressive wooden entry to the Willcox House.
- Sitting at dinner with Bonnie and Pat at the Selah Inn as Pat explains the challenges of maintaining the health of the beautiful Hood Canal.
- Feeling the warmth and openness of Kristy as she explains her motivation for buying The Villa and opening their lives to people from around the world.
- Arriving late at the El Gaucho Inn and having a perfectly prepared steak and bottle of Washington wine delivered to our room, so we did not have to leave our comfortable robes.
- Recommending The Sorrento Hotel to fussy out-of-town friends and having them rave about their stay.
- Taking the family on the Holland America cruise to Alaska and seeing the same headlands, waterfalls and glaciers that my grandfather saw when he sailed his own ship to Alaska in the early 1900's.
- Reserving a room at the Bellevue Club Hotel each year during the holidays so that our shopping spree can be followed by an "adults-only" vacation weekend.
- Looking down out the window in our room at the Salish at the spray coming up from the Snoqualmie River as it pours over the falls.
- Taking a break between courses at the Herbfarm to walk outside to feed Basel the resident pig and then looking ahead to four more opulent courses during dinner.
- Watching a bald Eagle swoop down and snatch his next meal just yards away from our water-side room at the Boatyard Inn.
- Enjoying some of the sexiest bathrooms in the state at the Inn at Langley.
- Feeling so smug when others began the long drive home

after a day touring the tulip fields around La Conner as we retired to the Wild Iris and enjoy soaking in the hot tub rather than stewing on I-5.

- Discovering the Majestic Hotel so we no longer get up at the crack of dawn to make a morning ferry. Instead, we have a relaxing night at the hotel, a well-prepared dinner and a leisurely breakfast allowing us to arrive at the ferry relaxed rather than haggard.

- Leaving our car behind when we take the ferry to Friday Harbor, since the Tucker House, Harrison Suites and Friday Harbor House are all a easy walk from the ferry dock. Saving the ferry fee covers a good part of the cost of the stay.

- Solving a family dilemma by staying at the Lakedale Resort: the kids love to camp and stay in a tent and we don't. So we stay in luxury and comfort in the lodge and the kids have a secure campsite. We meet for activities and meals, each feeling justified in their decision.

- Watching Bill and Susan at Turtleback Farm dispense the same gracious hospitality as they did 20-years ago.

- Enjoying the incredible dinner at the Inn at Ship Bay while watching the sun set across the water.

- Seeing the joy and pride in Jim's face as he describes how he and his family build each of the Bayside Cottages.

- Marveling with a sense of awe at the soaring lobby in the Chrysalis Inn.

- Listening to Riley at the Willows Inn explain how they grow their own organic foods and catch the salmon we just had for dinner—as if everyone did the same thing.

- Observing Renee quietly telling her guests at the Abendblume Pension how to get the most from their visit to Leavenworth.

- Sitting on the deck at Run of The River and relaxing by simply watching the river flow past.

- Taking the snow-cat up the snow covered mountain and emerging at Mountain Home Lodge surrounded by snow-capped peaks.

- Finishing a scenic horseback ride at Sun Mountain Lodge and recovering in their outdoor hot tub.

- Having the fortitude to tackle the famous Callebaut chocolate desert at Birchfield Manor.

- Realizing that we just stayed in the same room at the Marcus Whitman Hotel where Dwight and Mamie Eisenhower had stayed.

- Finding the new Fat Duck Inn and wanting to bring our friends here immediately.

- Marveling at the incredible workmanship that went into the creation of the main Lodge at Basel Cellars.

- Sitting in the impressive lobby at the Davenport Hotel and realizing this came so close to being lost to us all if not for the efforts of Walt and Karen Worthy.

- Looking up through the central atrium in the Montvale Hotel and seeing the cute faces of my daughter and wife looking down from the top floor.

During the past 23-years of publishing travel books, our goal has always been to help our readers become travelers and not tourists. This year, we are taking another major step by creating the *Association of Special Traveler*s.

The Association is designed for those travelers who want to get the most out of every trip; who want to be among the first to learn about a new inn, resort or hotel that is among the best of its type. And, it is for people who want to know more about a destination by reading comments from other Association members who have visited the area before them. The continuing goal is to help each member maximize their travel experience and never, ever be mistaken for a tourist.

MEMBER BENEFITS

As a member, you will have a password-controlled access to a "members only" section of the SpecialPlaces.com web site where you will find special offers from all the properties in each of our guidebooks. These special offers are created just for Association members and may involve significant savings for travel, or they may be packages that include exciting activities along with the lodging and meals. You can browse hundreds of offers and find the one that best matches your upcoming travel plans.

In the members-only section you will be able to post your own recommendations for activities and restaurants in and around the featured properties and you can read the comments of other members. This community of travelers, who love to find special places to stay, dine and recreate will be wonderful assets in helping other members get the most out of every trip.

The open portion of the web site will contain a limited amount of information on each of the selected Special Places, while the members section will have the complete editorial and the comments from other members.

ASK US/ TELL US

We will provide members with an email address so that you can ask us what we know about a specific property, or what might be the best fit for you among several places. If you know of a property that you believe merits a personal visit from us, you will have direct access to our travel desk and after we visit a recommended property, we will let you know our impressions.

The First to Know

There will be drawings for free trips and other members-only rewards made available each year. Periodically we will send you an e-newsletter making you the "first-to-know" about new Special Places we have selected. We will never give any personal information you provide to the Association to any outside person or entity.

Cost to Join the Association

If you purchase a book from us through the web site, you will automatically become a member of the Association for a year. As part of the purchase, we will set you up to immediately start enjoying the Association benefits.

If you purchased a Special Places book from a retail store, the annual Association membership fee is $16.95. Come to the SpecialPlaces.com web site and follow the instructions on joining the Association.

Each year as you renew your membership directly with us, you will have your selection of any of the current Special Places books as an added benefit of maintaining your membership in the Association.

And there is more...

In addition to the special places to stay, we are expanding our books to cover the top wineries in Washington, Oregon and British Columbia for touring and tasting. These wineries will also be including special offers to you on the members section. You may receive a free tasting, or special direct purchasing opportunities.

To continue to make the Association a valued membership for you, we will be adding properties in other parts of the western states and provinces where we do not plan to publish guidebooks. As an example, we may find 8-10 Special Places in Montana, not enough to publish a book, but of potential interest to our members. When I find such qualified properties, our members will learn about them first in the newsletter and then they will be included on the web site with their special offers for you. Association benefits will continue to expand as we identify like-quality places throughout the West.

The *Association of Special Travelers* is the only organization designed specifically for discerning travelers who want to know about special places to stay, to dine and to recreate. Each place is personally inspected by us before they are included in any of our publications or on the web site. Our members then have hundreds of enticing offers for lodging, dining or recreational activities. As a member you will be offered the best and never again have to wade through the rest.

Boatyard Inn

Inn at Port Hadlock

Bellevue Club

Sun Mountain Lodge

Inn at Shif

Shelburne Inn and China Beach Retreat

Too much of
a good thing
can be wonderful.
- Mae West

We hope you enjoy discovering the Special Places.

- Mardi & Fred Nystrom

www.SpecialPlaces.com

BOATYARD INN

To Order Additional Copies

For individual book orders

Please contact us using books@SpecialPlaces.com and for the $19.95 cost of the book, you will receive a year-long membership in the Association of Special Travelers at no additional charge.

As a Gift

When purchasing a book(s) as a gift, please let us know if you would like us to sign the book using your recipient's name. We can invoice you and ship the book directly to the recipient or to you. Please place all orders on the SpecialPlaces.com web site or by emailing us at giftbooks@SpecialPlaces.com

As a Fundraiser

If you would like to purchase and re-sell our books as a fundraiser for a group, please contact us at fundraising@SpecialPlaces.com and we will provide you with the outline of an entire fundraising program including the discounted prices of the books.

Run of the Riv

The Herbfarm

For the most up to date listing of Special Places—visit www.SpecialPlaces.com

This certificate is not to be redeemed unless it is attached to the book when presented for redemption. This certificate is not to be redeemed unless it is attached to the book when presented for redemption.

SPECIAL PLACES

We hope you enjoy discovering the Special Places

$10.00 Gift Certificate

Mardi & Fred Nystrom

Redeemed by: ____________________

Email address: ____________________

Date Redeemed: ____________________

Book purchased at: ____________________

This certificate may be redeemed at any of the properties featured in the 2007 *Special Places of Washington* book. The certificate is redeemable on a two-night stay.

This certificate is not to be redeemed unless it is attached to the book when presented for redemption. This certificate is not to be redeemed unless it is attached to the book when presented for redemption.

This certificate is not to be redeemed unless it is attached to the book when presented for redemption. This certificate is not to be redeemed unless it is attached to the book when presented for redemption.

SPECIAL PLACES

We hope you enjoy discovering the Special Places

$10.00 Gift Certificate

Mardi & Fred Nystrom

Redeemed by: ____________________

Email address: ____________________

Date Redeemed: ____________________

Book purchased at: ____________________

This certificate may be redeemed at any of the properties featured in the 2007 Special Places of Washington book. The certificate is redeemable on a two-night stay.

This certificate is not to be redeemed unless it is attached to the book when presented for redemption. This certificate is not to be redeemed unless it is attached to the book when presented for redemption.

SPECIAL PLACES

This certificate may only be used at properties featured in the 2007 Special Places of Washington book. The certificates expire June 1, 2009.

A certificate is to be redeemed on a two-night stay at the property where the certificate is presented.

The certificate must be attached to the book when presented. It is then to be completed and given to the property in order to receive the $10.00 credit on the room charge.

The certificate has no other value and may not be used for any other purpose.

SPECIAL PLACES

This certificate may only be used at properties featured in the 2007 Special Places of Washington book. The certificates expire June 1, 2009.

A certificate is to be redeemed on a two-night stay at the property where the certificate is presented.

The certificate must be attached to the book when presented. It is then to be completed and given to the property in order to receive the $10.00 credit on the room charge.

The certificate has no other value and may not be used for any other purpose.